Shaman Pathways

Elen of the Ways

Following the Deer Trods,
the Ancient Shamanism of Britain

Shaman Pathways

Elen of the Ways

Following the Deer Trods,
the Ancient Shamanism of Britain

Elen Sentier

MOON
BOOKS

Winchester, UK
Washington, USA

First published by Moon Books, 2013
Moon Books is an imprint of John Hunt Publishing Ltd., Laurel House, Station Approach,
Alresford, Hants, SO24 9JH, UK
office1@jhpbooks.net
www.johnhuntpublishing.com
www.moon-books.net

For distributor details and how to order please visit the 'Ordering' section on our website.

Text copyright: Elen Sentier 2013

ISBN: 978 1 78099 559 5

A CIP catalogue record for this book is available from the British Library.

Design: Stuart Davies
Cover photograph: David Kjaer

Printed and bound by CPI Group (UK) Ltd, Croydon, CR0 4YY

We operate a distinctive and ethical publishing philosophy in all
areas of our business, from our global network of authors to
production and worldwide distribution.

CONTENTS

About Elen Sentier   viii

Meetings   1

1.   Ice and Fire   3
    Our Deer-Trod Following Ancestors   4
    Deer and Humans   10
    Migratory Tracks   13
    Time, Art & Imagination   14

2.   Goddess of the North Wind   16
    Boreal Forest
    Greece: the Cerynian Hind   17
    Mongolia: Flying Deer Stones   19
    Sami Traditions   20

3.   Sovereignty   22
    The Dream of Macsen Wledig   23
    Antlered Goddess   24
    The Wild Hunt   26
    Quicksilver threads   28

4.   The Deer Goddess of the Ancient Caledonians   31
    Bean-Sìdhe & Giantesses
    Deer-Priestesses   33

5.   2012 Scotland   35
    Curlews & Light
    Assynt – Meadow of Stags   36
    Deer Alchemy   40
    Pig Land   41
    South Ronaldsay

Maeshowe   44
Stones of Stenness   45
Barnhouse Village   46
Ness of Brodgar   48
Ring of Brodgar
Skara Brae   50
Sea & Sky   51
Hoy Day   52
Journey: The Crossing   54
Reality, Spirit & Death   55
Journey: Death   57

6. Following the Deer Trods   60
   Growing up with Elen
   Walking Between Worlds   63
   Listening to the Elders   66

7. Deer Stalking – Working with Elen   67
   Spirit Keeper
   Bushcraft   69
   Finding Your Way
   Tracking   72
   Animal Tracks and Sign   73
   Tracking and being Awenydd   75
   Journey-work   76
   Non-Human Neighbours   77
   Ancestral Nous & Spirits of Place   78
   Getting to Know the Ancestors   79

Table of Figures

Figure 1: Swimming Reindeer   3
Figure 2: Lascaux Megaloceros   10
Figure 3: Boreal Forest   16
Figure 4: Cairngorm reindeer   17

Figure 5: Heracles & the Cerynian Hind — 18
Figure 6: Flying Deer of Mongolia — 19
Figure 7: Flying Deer Stones — 19
Figure 8: Romano-Gallic Figure — 25
Figure 9: Kite Wagon, Fiona, sunrise in Glencoe — 35
Figure 10: Antler at Banks Tomb — 43
Figure 11: Stones of Stenness — 45
Figure 12: Obvious Balance — 45
Figure 13: Balance? — 46
Figure 14: Barnhouse Structure Eight — 47

About Elen Sentier

I'm awenydd, a spirit keeper and taleweaver from a long family lineage. My mother's mother was a witch from the Isle of Man and my father was a taleweaver and awenydd whose family were closely involved with Annie Besant and Rudolf Steiner. I was born on Dartmoor, grew up on the edge of Exmoor and now live (with husband, cats and wildlife) in the back of beyond by the river Wye in the Welsh Marches where I write and teach the way of the awenydd, British native shamanism.

As well as my family and the wise women of the village where I grew up, various folk have helped me along the way including Tom Graves, Dr Don Robbins, Colin Bloy, Hamish Miller, Paul Broadhurst, Michael Poynder, Caitlin & John Matthews, Barbara Somers & Ian Gordon Brown of the Transpersonal, Caroline Wise, Cheska Potter, Paul Devereux and Fiona Dove. It has been, and still is, a lifelong journey for me. I hope this book will encourage you to discover and walk the quicksilver paths of Elen of the Ways for yourself. My website is http://www.elensentier.co.uk.

Meetings ...

I first met Elen of the Ways in the flesh many, many years ago back in the 1960s. I was at university and had come up to Exmoor to chill for the weekend, wild camping and walking my beloved woods. On the Saturday I went down to the Barle and after crossing the dragon-bridge I turned into the woods. I walked the river bank to the seven stepping stones over the Westwater – it's a nice new clapper bridge nowadays but then it was seven huge stepping stones. I crossed over and felt a real pull to go up the little valley into Westwater Copse.

After about half a mile I came to a glade ... and there she was, a red deer hind, heavily pregnant. I stood stock still, holding my breath. She had come here to drop her fawn.

'Am I in your way, shall I go?' I whispered.

There was a buzzing in my head, like a bee, and then I *saw* the words, flickering like lightning in my mind.

'You may stay,' she told me.

I stayed, watching.

Her belly strained, it seemed to take no time at all and all the time in the world, then there was a rush and the slippery fish of a baby deer fell into the soft grass. Immediately, the hind turned to lick the calf and soon the little one was struggling to her feet, wobbly, wondering where she was, how she would manage, but making it. Then she went to suck.

The hind looked at me over her shoulder. Again the buzzing, the flashing words.

'Go now, you have seen, remember! Remember me! Work for me!'

I nodded my head in salute to her and backed out of the grove. I'm not sure my feet actually touched the ground on the return journey down the hill, across the stepping stones, through the woods and back over the dragon bridge. It all seemed to take forever and yet no time at all ... but I was changed.

Elen of the Ways has been my mentor, teacher and guiding spirit all my life. She's always here; always her spirit is with me, to call on if I need. I often come across deer when I'm out walking in the wild places, they call me, speak to me, lead me along the deer-trods.

I

Ice and Fire

Long ago and far away in space-time ice covered the Earth. It would feel strange to us now, we who live in a warm time when snow only comes for a few weeks in winter, if at all.

In northerly climes like Scandinavia, parts of Russia, Canada and America, snow may come for several months over the winter but we have to go up into Arctic to find snow all the year round, and those lands are shrinking every year now because of global warming and climate change. We watch wonderful programmes like Frozen Planet but we cannot imagine living there. If we really stretch the imagination, our mind tells us that such an existence would be terrible, frightening, cold and miserable. We admire the explorers and scientists who go there for many months at a time but we do not believe the frozen wastes to be places to live, to make great art and philosophy; we consider them to be too bitterly cold to even think. Our ancestors didn't share these feelings as this beautiful carving shows.

Figure 1: Swimming Reindeer

This sculpture, known as the Swimming Reindeer, was created *at least* 13,000 years ago, that's three thousand years before the end of the last Ice Age. It's carved from the tip of a mammoth tusk and shows a male and female reindeer with their heads raised and legs extended. The depiction is remarkable in its naturalism;

it conveys movement and displays the hunter's knowledge of anatomy. It was discovered in 1866 as two separate pieces and acquired by the British Museum in 1887.

The fragility of the connection between the two halves shows that it was not a practical object but rather a masterpiece of figurative art. Its significance to the people who created it remains a mystery to archaeologists. For me, it is one of many things which tell me the Reindeer Goddess was important to humankind from back into very ancient times.

If we wanted to have this made for us now it would need craft-skills of superb delicacy as well as an exquisite visionary talent ... but it was made when the Earth was deep in an Ice Age. Our ancestors were not savages as was the perceived academic wisdom until quite recently; they were people of amazing culture which must, from the intricacy of such art, have had great spiritual depth. There are not many artists nowadays who could achieve such an evocative and skilled piece of work.

What would it be like to live the life of these people? How did they see the world and know the gods, the powers, and their elder brethren – the animals and plants and rocks?

Our Deer-Trod Following Ancestors

Reindeer have been around for a long time.

Wild reindeer have been a major resource for humans throughout the northernmost parts of the northern hemisphere for tens of thousands of years, from the Middle Pleistocene. Norway and Greenland have unbroken traditions of hunting wild reindeer from the ice age up to the present day. In the non-forested mountains of central Norway you can find the remains of stone trapping pits, guiding fences, and bow rests built especially for hunting reindeer, that have likely been in use since the Stone Age.

In the North American continent reindeer are called caribou. Caribou is an important source of food, clothing, shelter and tools in the traditional lifestyle of the Inuit people, Northern First Nations people, Alaska Natives, and the Kalaallit people of Greenland. Many Gwich'in people, who depend on the Porcupine caribou, still follow traditional ways of caribou management. These folk still follow the old ways that are similar to hunter-gatherer and pastoralist paths.

Before farming, the land was owned by none; it was known to be for all, all life belonged to the Earth, including all animal, plant and mineral life as well as humans. The concept of *ownership* began with farming.

Hunting and gathering was the ancestral way of life for humans for most of the six million years of our evolution from apes. It began to change about 10,000 years ago when agriculture began; before that all modern humans, homo sapiens, were hunter-gatherers. It was a very different way of life to what we know now as largely citified humans. Over the next few thousand years hunter-gatherers were displaced by farmers and, to some extent, by pastoralist groups in most parts of the world. Only a few contemporary societies are still able to be hunter-gatherers and many of those supplement foraging with keeping or following animals.

Life was good for the hunter-gatherers. Palaeolithic hunter-gatherer people didn't suffer from famine and malnutrition like the Neolithic farming tribes that followed them because they had access to a far wider variety of plants and animals and fish. The famines experienced by both Neolithic and modern farmers were and are caused, and intensified, by their dependence on a small number of crops. The Palaeolithic hunter-gatherers didn't suffer the modern diseases of affluence either, diseases such as Type 2 diabetes, coronary heart disease and cerebrovascular disease, because they ate mostly lean meats and plants, and engaged in lots of physical activity.

Archaeological evidence from the Dordogne region of France shows they used lunar calendars giving the phases of the moon.

Solar calendars do not appear until the Neolithic period. But our hunter-gatherer ancestors understood the seasons perfectly well, they knew how to follow the migration of animals like deer, and wild cattle and horses, far better than most of us do now.

At first, when the farmers began to take over and control the Earth, many hunter-gatherer groups continued their ways of life. Their numbers have continually declined as a result of pressure from growing agricultural and pastoral communities. As the number and size of agricultural societies increased, they expanded into lands traditionally used by hunter-gatherers, driving the hunter-gatherers out or forcing them to change into farmers. This process of agriculture-driven expansion led to the development of the first forms of what we know as modern government in agricultural centres such as the Fertile Crescent, Ancient India, Ancient China, Olmec, Sub-Saharan Africa and Norte Chico. The new farming societies also gave rise to the concept of war through the idea of ownership.

Many of the remaining hunter-gatherer societies now live in arid regions or tropical forests. Those areas which were formerly available to them were—and continue to be—encroached upon by the settlements of agriculturalists. The resulting competition for land use meant that hunter-gatherer societies either adopted farming or moved to other areas. Usually they were forced into lands much less suitable for their lifestyle and, in consequence, they became malnourished and sick, and so died out. According to American scientist and author Jared Diamond the ignorant practices of farmers, including overexploitation, caused many large mammal species to become extinct. This was further complicated in 19th century America by the idiotic romantic concept of "good animal" (pretty herbivore) and "bad animal" (wolf). The subsequent hunting of large predators which grew up wrecked the habitat balance which the hunter-gatherers and pastoralists had helped nature (the goddess) to maintain for millennia. Hunting wolves became a sort of religious war; it extends, still, to bears and big cats. The stupid and foolhardy modern destruction, such as began with the creation of the first National Park, Yellowstone, for material profit (i.e. tourism to line pockets) still goes on.

We see this still continuing today. Indeed there are still arguments over the reintroduction of wolves to Yellowstone although it has been proven that without wolves to balance their numbers the herbivores kill the forest. Intelligent scientists now realise how well the hunter-gatherer societies, who were thrown out of Yellowstone by the railway profiteers, worked with nature to maintain a proper ecological balance.

Another thing to note about hunter-gatherer society is that the division of labour was quite different to the way we have been taught to think of it. For our ancestors, man was not superior ... but neither was woman.

Back in 1966 at the "Man the Hunter" conference in Chicago, anthropologists Richard Borshay Lee and Irven DeVore made the (then) radical suggestion that *egalitarianism* was a major characteristic of nomadic hunter-gatherer societies. Being mobile, following the herds and the seasons, along with the efficient use of resources, knocks on the head all the ego-ideas of male superiority and female inferiority.

Personal material possessions were minimal, just what you needed to live and likely included only things such as a knife and axe, bow-drill hearth and maybe cord, a cookpot/carryall, and some form of "poncho" that you could use as a hammock or tarp. Collecting excess possessions was unhelpful, wasteful, greedy and unnecessary; to do so would be to steal from the land's own resources which other creatures and plants would need. Our ancestors were "ultralight backpackers". In their philosophy the *people belonged to the land*. It was only with the advent of farming that this concept was turned on its head to become the farmers' philosophy that people *owned* the land. This is a concept we are all familiar with nowadays. When following the herds, moving from place to place as the herds followed the seasons, was normal we knew our connectedness with the Earth and the goddess much more clearly than we do now. Grasping, greed, the fear of loss, the envy of another man's field, all these were concepts that had no place to exist before we decided to be owners and to control the Earth.

At the "Man the Hunter" conference, Marshall Sahlins presented a paper entitled *Notes on the Original Affluent Society* in which he challenged the popular view that hunter-gatherers lived lives that were *"solitary, poor, nasty, brutish and short"* as Thomas Hobbes had put it back in 1651. Sahlins showed that hunter-gatherers needed to work far fewer hours – now thought to be about 15 hours/week – than the later farmers in order to enjoy far more leisure than is nowadays typical for members of any industrial society. Hunter-gatherers ate well and seasonally, so their bodies were well nourished by what is best at each time of the year. Nowadays we have the rather childish attitudes of being overly fussy and wanting "treats" all the time, such as strawberries in midwinter. The hunter-gatherer *affluence* came about because they needed very little in the material sense in order to be content, and to produce beautiful art which is an expression of a deep philosophy … unlike us today.

Mutual exchange and sharing of resources, such as the meat gained from hunting or the berries harvested for preserving, wine and cordial, are important in hunter-gatherer societies. In our modern way of classifying, labelling and putting into boxes, we sometimes describe such practices as *gift economies* although we don't really understand the concept of gifting. Gifting is an ancient shamanic habit; we gift between each other, between ourselves and other tribes; we gift the land and receive gifts from the land; and we gift between worlds. It's a fundamental part of shamanic practice to gift back to the land and to Otherworld as well as to other people. This is another trait we have largely lost in modern society except at midwinter sun-return and birthdays.

There is a vast amount of ethnographic and archaeological evidence which demonstrates that the sexual division of labour in which men hunt and women gather wild fruits and vegetables is uncommon and unlikely among hunter-gatherers worldwide. The evidence suggests gathering is often done by women but no society has ever been found in which men completely abstain from gathering easily available plants. Often women hunt the small game while men tend to hunt the large game, likely because the human male torso has more strength than the female and men may have more stamina for a long running chase. But there are quite a few documented exceptions to this; for instance, in the Philippines, about 85% of Aeta women hunt, and they hunt the same quarry as men. Studies show that Aeta women hunt in groups, and with dogs, and have a 31% success rate as opposed to 17% for men; their rates are even better when they combine forces with men. The Jul'hoansi women in Namibia track the quarry for the men.

Recent archaeological research by anthropologist and archaeologist Steven Kuhn from the University of Arizona suggests that the sexual division of labour did not exist prior to the Upper Paleolithic. It seems to have developed very recently in human history, probably with the beginning of land-ownership. The idea that sexual division of labour arose to allow humans to acquire food and other resources more efficiently is a myth, likely instigated by power/land/property struggles rather than for any life-enhancing reasons.

As a result of the now near-universal human reliance upon agriculture, the few contemporary hunter-gatherer cultures are only able to live in areas the farmers consider unsuitable for agricultural use. This change in how we work – with each other as well as with the Earth – has brought us to a place where one sex dominates the other. We have lost our way ... we no longer follow the deer-trods.

Deer and Humans

The earliest fossil deer were found in Europe and date from about 34 million years ago.

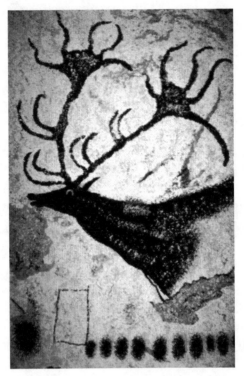

Figure 2: Lascaux Megaloceros

This exquisite Lascaux cave painting is of the Irish Elk, *Megaloceros giganteus* who first appeared about 400,000 years ago, that's in the time of archaic Homo sapiens ancestors. This gigantic deer stood over two metres tall at the shoulder, that's nearly seven foot in old money, they had the largest antlers of any known deer at over three and a half metres from tip to tip and weighed in at maybe 600 kg. There's an impressive and significant collection of Irish Elk skeletons at the Natural History Museum in Dublin.

The Lascaux painting is quite stunning and shows how very

well our ancestors knew deer. It was painted on the wall of a cave in southern France, far underground and hidden from everyday sight. To see it you made a journey into the womb of the Earth, in darkness; then, with the flame-lights lit, you would stand in the presence of the Deer Spirit.

Undoubtedly we ate these deer, the butchered bones in caves all over Britain and Europe attest to this. Archaeologists suggest the paintings were a form of calling to the gods for help with the hunt and that's a part of it but there's more than that. Shamanic peoples know hunting and killing a beast is a sacred task, your beast will show itself to you, stop maybe, make it quite obvious that he or she is the one you should kill. People who live wild know this whether they are knowingly working with spirit or not, too many "odd things" happen so that you really feel you're pushing "coincidence" far too far. Unless you go out and experience this for yourself it can be hard for modern city folk to appreciate.

Shamanic people everywhere know the interconnectedness of all life ... and this means what you eat and what eats you too. Our bodies and those of animals and plants are all made of the same atoms that make up Mother Earth: the atoms that make up your skin and organs and brain have all been atoms of rock and cabbage and cat and motor car and concrete and other people etc, etc ... and they will be so again after you no longer need them. Spirit, your spirit, builds your body like a space-suit for living on Planet Earth out of the stuff of Earth. Your spirit then inhabits the space-suit for the duration of your incarnation and at the end, when your body dies, all the atoms go back into the Earth again to become other things.

When you're in touch with your spirit and, even more so, when you know yourself to be that spirit rather than just your little personal self you know this in your bones rather than in your head. It's all the stuff I was brought up with as normal and has been so for awenyddion, spirit keepers, for time out of mind.

Knowing this means you know to ask for permission to kill your food … and you kill a carrot every time you pull one up to eat it (or buy it in a shop) just as much as a cow or sheep of deer is killed so you can eat meat. You and the cow and the sheep and the deer and the carrot all share the same atoms; some of the stuff that currently makes up your body may well have been atoms in a deer and, when you die, some of your atoms may go on to be a carrot. As awenydd you know this; you respect all of life whatever its shape and form; and you know that we all nourish each other in a completely physical way, all the time.

I think these paintings are about all of that; a far more complex, and complete, idea of the world, the universe and everything.

We know our ancestors were not "ignorant savages" as earlier history books told us. We know they were complex and sophisticated people who knew very accurately where the sun rose and set on the horizon so they could build enormous and complex structures like Stonehenge, Maes Howe, Avebury and the myriad other ancient monuments to celebrate this. We know they were incredibly skilled and visionary artists. Their concept of the Earth and the universe was perhaps even more intricate and complete than any we know today; they certainly had time and leisure and good health to contemplate and build such an understanding. It's been known in science since the 1960s that our hunter-gatherer ancestors only needed to "work" about 15 hours a week to have a very good life. Ray Mears, the international wilderness expert, also showed us this in the BBC documentary television series "Wild Food" in which he and Professor Gordon Hillman, an expert in the use of plants, followed our ancestors' lifestyle and hunting techniques. And it was only after the introduction of agriculture that life became hard and the diseases of *work*, like arthritis, became prevalent.

The people who made the cave paintings knew about life, and they knew about spirit; it was normal, a part of everyday life, how you lived. The paintings were part of how they communicated with Otherworld and how they carried forward the lore. They were honouring and respecting the life which supported them and which they, in turn, supported and which was massively older than themselves and so had much wisdom to give ... if they asked, and the paintings are a form of asking too, as well as the answers.

Migratory Tracks

Our ancestors used the migration trails of the reindeer as part of their lives; even now there are still peoples, such as the Caribou People, who follow these age-old ways.

Animals make and use tracks and pathways across the land. Flocks and herds use these ancient roads until humans build some obstruction, road, farm, house, city, across them. Alaskans who built their towns on the polar bear routes now complain when the bears enter them. Similar things have happened in Africa where towns and cities have been built on the routes elephants or wildebeest have used for millennia on their treks across the continent. Our ancestors knew the old trails and would never build on them. Nowadays, most people no longer know how to ask, in the old way, if this is a place they should be; ever since settlements became the rule for human living, they try to control the non-human world to make it conform to human wants.

Reindeer have the *migration urge*, they know-in-their-bones the ancient tracks that lead them across the land from pasture to pasture according to the seasons. Reindeer may be *semi*-domesticated at the most. They not herded in the same way as other cattle, and those who live and work with them do so on the negotiated basis of equal wills rather than the *power-over* attitude of farmers. The Caribou-folk of the northern part of the American continent still follow the deer-trods quite literally; they still follow the herds in the ancient way of the hunter-gatherer.

Other folk follow the herds but also forage from the land around them. For instance, the Sami collect, gather and use herbs, berries, birch bark, plants and mushrooms, herbs and medicines from the land they live and through which their herds move from the land their herds use. They also fish and use sea, shore and river plants. Their culture relies on the animals for their meat as well as all the other things like sinew-cordage, clothing, shoes, covering for yurts and laavu. As Paul Kirtley of Frontier Bushcraft says, there is a misconception that pastoralists have no knowledge of the bush, the non-plains wilderness. This is a fallacy which, I suspect, comes from the modern syndrome of labelling and compartmentalising everything, i.e. pastoralists will have no idea of woodland because they rely on their animals. Such bland generalisations are convenient to lazy thinkers but perpetrate a false idea of reality.

The Sami society cannot strictly be described as hunter-gatherers; according to perceived wisdom a hunter-gatherer society is one in which most if not all food is obtained from wild plants and animals. As the Sami live and *work with* the reindeer they do not fit into that box whereas the Caribou folk do because the herds are quite wild. The Mongolian reindeer people are like the Sami living with the beasts as they follow them from pasture to pasture; both they and the Sami live as part of the herd. Even now, when the Sami have settled, fixed, homes they still go out with the herds. Nowadays they use snow-mobiles and dogs whereas, in the old days, they would have followed the animals on skis. They take it in turns, in the family, to go wandering for a few weeks with the reindeer rather than spending all their lives out with them in the nomadic way their ancestors used to do. But they still *journey* and follow the reindeer paths.

Time, Art & Imagination

Our ancestors had time and a very good lifestyle, one that could easily support such artistry as produced the Swimming Reindeer.

This lifestyle would also support the depth of thought and philosophy behind such wonderful art.

We know now that the Neanderthals also were skilled crafts-folk. During the excavations at Belvedere of 1981-1991 Professor Wil Roebroeks, Professor of Archaeology at Leiden University discovered the Neanderthals used iron oxides to create pigments and they used these pigments artistically. The old "Ugg! Ugg!" concept of our Neanderthal ancestors was very far outside the mark. Roebroeks and his colleagues made their discovery when they were investigating very tiny specks of red powder found in excavations at Maastricht-Belvédère. The red ochre in the material from Maastricht was found to contain haematite, a mineral that contains iron oxide; as haematite did not occur in that area it must have been imported from elsewhere, perhaps many miles away. The fact that the metals were imported tells us our ancestors knew about the world, how big it was, about trading, things we had thought they had no concept for.

Our ancient ancestors were wonderfully skilled artists with time to think and ponder, dream and journey, well able to visualise ideas and make connections, to learn and know the deep links with the Earth.

2

Goddess of the North Wind

Boreal Forest

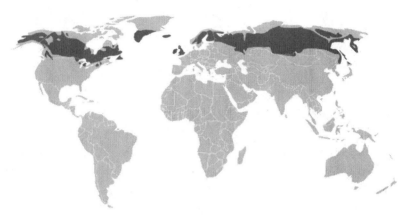

Figure 3: Boreal Forest

The *Boreal Forest* is the largest forest on Earth, the world's biggest terrestrial biome making up 29% of the world's forest. It extends all around the northern end of the world through Sweden, Finland, Norway, across Asia to the Pacific Ocean, including much of Siberia, northern Kazakhstan and Mongolia and the northern Japanese island of Hokkaidō. In North America it's called the Northwoods and covers most of inland Canada and Alaska as well as parts of the northern United States. It even includes the northern part of Iceland. It runs everywhere from the Tundra at latitude 70° to the southern tip of Cornwall at latitude 50° ... Britain was part of the Boreal Forest, our old woods like the Caledonian forest, the moors and wild places in Wales and England, and the Highlands of Scotland are all that's left.

Figure 4: Cairngorm reindeer

The ancient Greeks called the north wind Boreas and they called Britain *Hyperborea*, meaning *the land behind the North Wind*; we British were the *Hyperboreans*. Reindeer were native to our land long ago and they are now coming back through the wild herds in the Cairngorms. The Boreal Forest was the world of the reindeer; they thrive here. Our ancestors followed the deer trods and knew Elen of the Ways.

Greece: the Cerynian Hind

The reindeer mythos spread further south than the climatic limits of the Boreal Forest, down into ancient Greece. Pictures of a female deer bearing antlers and being caught by the hero Heracles are on several pieces of Greek art. Both pictures and story suggest reindeer, the only female deer to carry antlers. Robert Graves thought the myth related to Hyperborea.

The tale is of a beautiful, female deer sacred to Artemis, with golden antlers and hooves of bronze, who could outrun an arrow in flight. As one of his labours, Heracles has to capture and deliver her to his patron, Eurystheus. Heracles finds and chases her across Greece for the magical year-and-a-day. Eventually she

Figure 5: Heracles & the Cerynian Hind

comes to the river Ladon where Heracles shoots and immobilises her. On his way to Eurystheus, Heracles meets Artemis and her brother Apollo. Eurystheus hoped this would happen and that Artemis would punish Heracles for stealing her sacred hind. Heracles explains the situation and promises to return the deer when his task is done. Artemis forgives Heracles and heals the deer's wound. Heracles takes the hind to his master but says Eurystheus must come to get her himself. Eurystheus comes and, as he does, Heracles releases the deer who turns and runs faster than an arrow back to Artemis.

Like so many Celtic teaching tales, this is a riddling story where obligations are indeed fulfilled but not as originally expected. The big lesson in them is to go into the adventure full of expectancy but with no expectations or preconceptions of how it will turn out!

Mongolia: Flying Deer Stones

The southern edge of the Boreal Forest includes northern Mongolia. Around Lake Baikal, the Sayan and Altai Mountain regions, in Kazakstan, in Orenburg and Kavkasia, and near the Elba River are the Flying Deer Stones. They are, perhaps, the most beautiful still extant objects of deer reverence. The stones are carved with reindeer pictures and date from the Bronze and Early Iron Ages about three to five thousand years old.

Figure 6: Flying Deer of Mongolia

Figure 7: Flying Deer Stones

Although archaeologists have been researching the deer stones for over a hundred years they know very little about their meaning or why they were made and placed where they are.

The carvings on the stones are divided into three sections representing the sky, the earth and the underworld; this way of seeing the world is common among shamanic traditions.

- The top of most stones is carved with one or two large, and one or more smaller, round rings. Beneath them are smaller geometric forms. Upperworld is often described by a circle and holds the two lights, the sun and moon.

- The midsection of the stone, between Upperworld and Lowerworld, has the flying deer carvings, and those of other hooved animals, usually in profile.
- The lower part of the stone is often a cross-hatched border, like a belt, with weapons, tools, bows, arrows and other motifs like chevrons hanging from it.

Flying antlered deer are part of the mythos of the Boreal Forest and are still part of the spirit-lives of Tsaatan reindeer herders of Northern Mongolia who know that animals carry the spirits of the dead across the worlds. This is similar to the stories of the Scottish Highlands and to my own upbringing.

Sami Traditions

Sieidis, Seita or Storjunkare, (depending on local dialect) are the sacred places of the Sami. They occur where there are unusual landforms. Some are made of unusually shaped stones or they might be as simple as a tree stump or even just a pole. They are gifted with the hide and hooves of reindeer. It is said that a stone taken from such a place will grow lighter when the bearer guesses what the place wants – another common asking practice, asking the Land, the goddess, what she needs rather than imposing our own ideas on her.

Each Sami family or clan has its own Sieidis in the area where they live; some individuals have their own Sieidis too. They might be near caves, hunting grounds or fishing places, or on a mountain. They are *spirit focal points* and *gateways* to the spirit world as are our own sacred places, stone circles and caves.

Where there are reindeer their skins will be used to make the drums and their sinews to make the tension strings and hold the hides to the frame of the drum; the beater is carved from reindeer bone. Both drum and beater are decorated with symbols.

The *noaidi* can be a woman or a man. The drum is their steed, the reindeer who carries them across the worlds. The *noaidi* shapeshift and take another form, maybe that of a wild reindeer in whose shape they fly in the sky, or go deep underground or swim the rivers. Like shamans all over the world, they travel to the lands of the ancestors and the places of the gods in order to learn and bring back wisdom for their people.

3

Sovereignty

In the British Celtic tradition the goddess is the Earth and the Land, the god is the guardian of the Earth and the husbandman of the Land.

The goddess is known to us as *Sovereignty*. It is not the god who rules with the goddess subservient but the other way around; the goddess *holds* the power while the god *serves* and is *guardian of* the power. Amongst the reindeer it is the old grandmother deer who knows the ways and leads the herd to knew pastures according to the season.

We are well used to the idea of male deer fighting between themselves for whose genes will go forward each autumn but have you ever watched the rut? The female deer collect around the (currently) strongest male; they watch and wait to see who will turn out to be the best guardian for the herd and so whose genes will best serve the needs of the herd.

In the old lore-stories the male hero struggles and fights to be the one to wed the queen, princess or goddess – the story of Macsen searching for his dream princess, Elen, is one of these, or the story of Culhwch and Olwen. It's in our songs too; The Coal Black Smith is one of the best known depicting the chase that the goddess sets up in order to test whether the god is sufficiently wise, cunning and capable to be her guardian. It's a shifter-song too, both goddess and god shift into many different forms until, eventually, the goddess achieves her aim of bedding with the god, *allowing* him to catch her. In recent times this song has been degraded into a rape song which is a million miles from the truth; the goddess tests the god to see if he is up for the job of Guardian.

Remember the deer ... the females waiting and watching to see which stag will prove the wisest, most canny and cunning, strongest and best able to father the new generation. I've watched the red deer rut many times on Exmoor. One time, while two magnificent stags were pushing and shoving, fighting to prove themselves the best, a little side-drama happened. Down wind and out of sight of the big stags was a young male with only a small rack of antlers courting a couple of young females. He succeeded in luring them to a spot hidden from the big stags where he mounted each of them in turn, thus ensuring his genes would continue. The females approved his cunning and guile, considering them useful attributes to pass on.

The goddess does the same; she sets up tests to see if her man is able to keep up with her, be useful to her. The people who followed the deer also followed the deer's ways; they *enabled* the female members of the tribe and ensured the males knew their essential role as guardian.

The Dream of Macsen Wledig

This is the story of Elen. It's in the Mabinogion, a collection of lore-stories brought together by Lady Charlotte Guest and the Rhys-Jones brothers. The tales are wonderful, strange, tortuous and complicated. Our forebears spoke in riddles; in Ireland today some people still say, "I'll riddle you" as a caution. In the tales, particularly in Culhwch and Olwen, riddling is sometimes called *crying satire* on a person; the satirist, as do our reporters today, tells mockery, irony, parody and lampoon on the person they threaten or expose. It was often done in riddles rather like some of what are now our nursery rhymes – the Grand Old Duke of York being one. You tell truth but in a hidden way, riddling.

The story of Macsen and Elen is a story of magic and, like all lore-stories, it tells us about the crossings between the worlds. Elen sends a dream to a potential guardian-husband to see if he can interpret it and find her. Macsen succeeds. The concept of the goddess testing the god to see if he is up to being her guardian runs through many of our British songs and stories. The Fith

Fath Song, the Twa Magicians and the Coal Black Smith all tell of the chase the goddess leads her potential mate; they are not tales of rape.

This is a story that teaches us about Sovereignty. Elen grants Macsen the kingship through her own right, because she is an otherworldly woman and Queen, he cannot be king without her. She is the Earth-spirit; he is he Guardian of the Earth.

It comes out in all our stories. The grail-cup is guarded and defended by the spear and sword. The cup is the symbol for the holding the vessel, the womb, the Earth herself; the spear or sword is the symbol for the phallus that defends and enlivens the womb. The Tao de Ching says it rather nicely when it speaks of the receptive and the creative; the receptive is the cup, the womb; the creative is the spear, the phallus. The principle of sovereignty goes all around the world.

We lost this concept gradually over the millennia. The loss speeded up enormously after the Norman conquest of Britain. This loss and the misconceptions it leaves us with have made it near impossible for us to understand how to *work with* the Earth, how to respect the goddess as sovereignty, how to ask her what she needs rather than knowing best and imposing on her. If we can find our way back to Elen's Ways again we may be able to put ourselves back on track.

Antlered Goddess

Elen of the Ways is the ancestral antlered goddess of Britain. Elen was the goddess who led us, through the reindeer herds, to safe living in both summer and winter.

We know from modern peoples who still follow the reindeer that you don't keep or work them like cattle, they can only partially be domesticated at the most ... they don't follow you, you follow them, as the Sami people still do. So did our ancestors here in Britain. Reindeer are led by the elder antlered matriarch of the herd; there are statues and carvings of the reindeer goddess across Europe as this Romano-Gallic figure shows.

Figure 8: Romano-Gallic Figure

Not much has come down to us from those times; indeed all the times before the Romans we call *pre-history* ... because there is little or no *extant writing* to tell us anything. If people used writing – and they must certainly have been clever enough to invent it judging from their exquisite art – then no trace of it has yet been found. If they used skins to write on this is quite under-standable; just because later peoples, perhaps like the Neolithic farmers, used stone to write on it doesn't mean our hunter-gatherer ancestors did. We are encouraged to see the invention of farming as a huge leap forward for humankind but this view should be pondered over very carefully rather than leaping to currently perceived wisdom. Farmers had increasingly arduous and busy lifestyles whereas our hunter-gatherer ancestors had only to "work" 15 hours a week. The beginning of farming also brought with it the beginning of the modern diseases we still suffer from now. It seems to me quite possible that the deep-knowing skills of our ancient ancestors got lost because the hard-working and painful lives of farmers leaves no space-time for pondering, contemplation and creativity. Our pre-farming ancestors were wonderful artists so they may also have used writing but, unfortunately, on perishable materials. We need to remember that the absence of evidence is *not* evidence of absence!

Such a people, with plenty of time to think and talk, meditate and journey, would learn many deep secrets that we are only just coming back to after some 10,000 years. Traces of the things they knew have come down to us through story and song but unfortunately many of these have been misinterpreted by people into human stories. Elen is not human. Variations on her name, *Elen*, turn up in places all around the northern world; for example *Elain* is Welsh for 'Fawn'; *Jelen* is Czech for deer. She is portrayed as an antlered deer goddess and reindeer are the *only* deer species in which females grow antlers. The beasts of the goddess still know the old paths that carry the energies of the land; these pathways are the threads that hold the balance and cycles of nature. They are the Ways of Elen.

The Wild Hunt

The Wild Hunt is part of our ancient folklore and the other half of Elen. The huntsman is her Guardian as Macsen is in that story.

The Wild Hunt is known across Europe as a phantasmal, ghostly, spectral group who ride horses and follow hounds in pursuit of something or someone. Often they ride across the skies, sometimes along the ground or seeming to be just above it.

Their leader has many names, depending on where the story is told. The Welsh psychopomp Gwyn ap Nudd is the one we often work with in Britain, sometimes as Herne the Hunter. I grew up with Gwyn as the goddess' guardian and he has always been a good friend. His hounds are white with red ears and eyes and will follow only him, they cannot be called off by anyone else.

Seeing the Wild Hunt was thought by Christians to presage some catastrophe like war, plague or the death of whoever beheld it. Those who tried to follow or got in the path of the Hunt might be kidnapped and brought to the land of the dead. Some people find their spirit is called during sleep to follow the hunt.

I know the Hunt well from working with Gwyn most of my life. There was one old woman in the village who especially worked with him and I was very attracted to her, would go and play and work with her from about eight years old. Some of the other children found her frightening, and she was no oil painting to look at, but I loved her. She followed Gwyn and would take me up onto our local hilltop to work. The wild geese would fly over us there in the autumn and she would say, 'Here they come! Look! Here are the wild geese!' She would tell me the stories about how the hounds would shapeshift into the geese to fly north for the winter. Sometimes a goose would come down to her, she would stroke the bird and talk with it – if you know Canada geese you'll know they can be very fierce! She was never bitten or hurt by them and nor was I. She would come back to the village with wisdom.

Gwyn's hounds, in whatever shape they come, are fierce and wild but will be very good friends and wonderful guardians if you take the time to get to know them, indeed there've been several times when they've protected me from quite serious situations. I've asked them to guard other folk who've come to me needing help and they always do. Quite often the people I'm working with hear and see them to. I never properly describe them before the work but afterwards people will come back to me with perfect pictures of the hounds and although they realise how fierce they are they're not frightened by them, not even the children.

The Wild Hunt is seen in many places around Britain including Cadbury Castle in Somerset, Glastonbury Tor,

Dunkery Beacon on Exmoor and my own local one of Wild Edric at the Stiperstones. In my birth-county of Devon the hounds are known as Yeth (Heath) or Wisht Hounds and the hunt is particularly associated with Wistman's Wood on Dartmoor near where I was born. In Cornwall it's the Dandy Dogs; in Wales they are the Cwn Annwn, the Hounds of Annwn, lord of the Underworld; in Somerset they are Gabriel Ratchets or Retchets, which means dogs; there is also the name *Herlaþing* which is Old English for Herla's assembly. The Hunt is seen most often in the autumn and winter, the time of the Hunter's Moon, as we go down to Samhain and the season of death and rebirth.

In North America the Wild Hunt are called the Ghost Riders. In Europe it has many names including the *Mesnée d'Hellequin* meaning the household of Hellequin in old North French: *divoký hon* or *štvaní* which is Czech for wild hunt: *Dziki Gon* or *Dziki Łów* in Polish: *Oskoreia* or *Åsgårdsreia* in Norwegian meaning the ride of Asgard: *Estantiga* from Hoste Antiga meaning the old army, and *Hostia, Compaña* and *Santa Compaña* meaning troop or company in Galicia: *güestia* in Asturia. In Germany the Hunt is *Wilde Jagd* meaning wild hunt/chase or *Wildes Heer* meaning wild army.

The best known image of an antlered deer god appears on the Gundestrup cauldron and often holds the name of Cerrunos; another form of Gwyn ap Nudd.

Quicksilver threads

Elen guards the quicksilver threads, energy lines, magical pathways that stretch across the sacred Isle of Britain connecting sacred wells, stone circles, quoits, dolmens, hilltops and other sacred sites and yet she is virtually unknown in Britain. These threads are the energy roads that the Wild Hunt travels along.

Some are lych or lyke roads, corpse roads, spirit paths that the souls of the dead travel to Otherworld. They are also roads the corpses were carried along to burial, or the pyre, or up to a sky-platform. Elen's guardian has a role as psychopomp, guiding spirits homewards between the worlds. The Welsh still revere Elen as *Elen of the Roads* who at Beltane (1st May) opens the roads to travellers.

In the Dream of Macsen Wledig, Elen asks for three caers to be built for her, as her bride-gift. She goes on to build a network of magical roads between them that are called the Sarn Elens. They are similar to Watkins' ancient trackways that join together ancient sites like tumuli, burial mounds, hillforts, stone circles and so on. Elen is the guardian of these.

On 30th June 1921, Alfred Watkins was at Blackwardine, a village just up the road from where I live in Herefordshire. He was looking at a map with no particular object in mind when he noticed an alignment that passed over some hilltops and various ancient sites. All of a sudden he had a flash of insight, seeing the features so familiar to him in the local landscape become linked into a whole system. Allen Watkins, in a biography of his father, describes how his father's mind was *"...flooded with a rush of images forming one coherent plan. The scales fell from his eyes and he saw that over many long years of prehistory trackways were in straight lines marked out by experts on a sighting system. The whole plan of the Old Straight Track stood suddenly revealed"*.

Alfred Watkins later described this plan ...

Imagine a fairy chain stretched from mountain peak to mountain peak, as far as the eye could reach, and paid out till it touched the high places of the earth at a number of ridges, banks and knowls. Then visualise a mound, circular earthwork, or clump of trees, planted on these high points, and in low points in the valley, other mounds ringed with water to be seen from a distance. Then great standing stones brought to mark the way at intervals, and on a bank leading up to a mountain ridge or down to a ford the track cuts so deep so as to form a guiding notch in the skyline as you come up. In a bwlch or mountain pass the road cut deeply to show as a notch afar off. Here and there, and at two ends of the way, a beaconfire used to lay out the track. With

ponds dug on the line, or streams banked up into "flashes" to form
reflecting points on the beacon track so it might be checked when at least
once a year a beacon was fired on the traditional day. All these works
exactly on the sighting line ...

John Michell describes Watkins' experience as one when "the
barrier of time melted and, spread across the country ...".

I began working with ley lines back in the early 1970s, meeting
Paul Devereux, Colin Bloy, Michael Poynder and many others
who followed the path. Work on the Dragon Project with Dr Don
Robbins showed me that there are curved and multiple-threaded
lines as well as the straight ones. Elen's threads twist and wind
through the land along with the rivers and streams, and the paths
that animals take – they follow the earth-energies. The paths may
also follow geological lines, patterns where one form of rock sits
against another; sometimes this shows where ancient boundaries
occurred, demarking places guardianed by large spirits of place.

4

The Deer Goddess of the Ancient Caledonians

In November 1930 historian JG McKay gave a seminal talk on the deer goddess cult of the ancient Caledonians. He had pulled together a great mass of tales, traditions and customs to show that, in the Highlands of Scotland, the deer goddess led the way. In fact he suggests a common deer-cult through Europe. He was on the right track as we now know that deer, particularly reindeer, are revered across the lands of the Boreal Forest.

Bean-Sìdhe & Giantesses

McKay shows us the mysterious feminine characters in the old Gaelic tales who often appear as colossal Old Women. He found that, with one exception, they are all local, spirits of place; they owned, herded, and milked the deer of their respective districts; and that deer are the "fairy cattle".

The Scottish Highlands, like all the non-citified places of Britain, are peopled by the *Sidhe* who en-spirit the trees, bushes, rivers, rocks, caves, mounds and mountains of the land. McKay calls them *canny* which means cunning, shrewd, wily and crafty; he also calls them *uncanny* meaning eerie, weird, mysterious and strange. The awenyddion are all these things too.

Modern folk tend to think of fairies as being small and pretty. It's worth looking at the "faerie paintings" of artists like John Anster Fitzgerald, Richard Dadd and Arthur Rackham who all "painted from life". Their pictures show us the un-cute side of the Faer folk. McKay found the Sidhe could be "a colossal old deer-goddess as well as a tiny green fairy woman"; they were known as *bean-sidhe*.

Deer, fairy cattle, are always in the care of the feminine, never the masculine. It is the women and the goddess – Sovereignty – who own, herd and milk the deer, and dote on them. The fairy woman transforms herself into a red-deer. For us, down south on Dartmoor and Exmoor, it was an antlered female deer, taking us back again to reindeer.

The bean-sìdhe are spirits-of-place, called the Cailleach or sometimes Cailleach Mhor (Huge Old Woman) of the local ben, strath, river, or district. They are all gigantic, the most tremendous creatures of Gaelic myth; giantesses who sing to their deer, call them "darling deer" and "beast of my love". They are the *mistresses* of the deer.

Later tales tell that they come to dislike hunters because the hunters make selfish depredations on the herds without asking the goddess for her permission to hunt. It's likely this dates from times when deer herds dwindled as the forests were cleared for agriculture.

Our hunter-gatherer ancestors always *worked with* the deer-guardians. The rituals were *not* about appeasing but about *asking* and *being shown* which beasts they could kill; they took only what was needed for the health of the herds as well as for the people. This is real ecological balance, considering the needs of the prey as well as the needs of the hunter.

The goddess is seen as benevolent. She will not harm the hunters unless they provoke her. The folk memories clearly distinguish between the benevolent deer-goddesses and the general run of Gaelic giantesses who are often ferocious and cannibalistic. The word for giantess, ban-fhuamhair, is never applied to the huge deer-goddess. The bean-sìdhe, the gigantic Old Women, love their deer, they are Deer-Goddesses.

None of the Highland Deer-Goddesses shows any sign of domestication. Not one of the deer-goddesses wields distaff, pitchfork or broom; they are all creatures of the wild which, as McKay says, suggests great antiquity – and I'm thinking they go back to Palaeolithic times. Their tales are simple and read like chapters in natural history, they are not like modern and human-oriented stories which have a series of adventures, events and a plot leading up to a climax.

And ... there are no stories of *male* giants associated with deer.

The Irish An Chailleach Bhearach, The Old Woman of Beare, assumes deer-shape in order to lead Fionn (Fingal) into a trap. In his poem (which is likely based on old tales) Dean Swift says the Cailleach rode in a chariot drawn by four elks with golden horns. The elk or wapiti is one of the largest species of deer in the world. Elk used to be thought of as a subspecies of the European red deer but evidence from a study of the mitochondrial DNA, in 2004, indicates that they are different species. In the old days they would be known as deer.

It seems An Chailleach Bhearach came to Scotland from Ireland where she became Cailleach Bheur or Cailleach Bheurr and intimately connected with the deer unlike her Irish counterpart who stuck to shapeshifting into deer-shape.

Deer-Priestesses

The 19th century Orkney folklorist, Walter Traill Dennison, called the Orcadian wise-woman the *spaewife*. She was skilled in medicine and surgery, in dreams, in foresight and second-sight, and was well-regarded in her local community. They were healers, midwives and the women who did the laying out of the dead. The spaewife sounds just like the wise women who taught me in my childhood.

On the mainland, in the Highlands, she would be called *Glaistig*. Hunters knew the deer are the goddess' own cattle and a part of her spirit and would visit the wise woman to ask her blessing on the hunt. On their return, they would share the game with her and there would be some piece for the goddess herself; they would share the rest with the tribe.

The old ways likely began to be corrupted with the beginnings of the concept of "ownership of land" which didn't exist before farming. Our ancestors knew they belonged to the land rather than it belonging to them, as the shamanic folk everywhere still do. Even when I was growing up in the 1950s there was still the idea that the farmers were guardians of the land and that it should stay in the family because that family had made a promise to the land in return for livelihood. That seems almost gone now. Nowadays everyone wants to "own", to "have a piece of the action". For the hunter-gatherer it would be utterly wrong to own; everything was shared with the land, the goddess, sovereignty and the tribe. We have lost this concept in modern life.

The Green Isle, the Happy Isles, the Isles of the Dead, whichever name you use, all grew very special apples; those who ate the apples instantly grew deer's antlers, fully matured, from out of their heads. Eating other apples from the island caused the antlers to fall off again just as instantly. This harks back for me to the stories we children were told on the edge of both Dartmoor and Exmoor when I was growing up there back in the 1950s. Carolyn Hillier, the musician and drum-maker who lives on Dartmoor, has a lovely version of this that you can read on her website; it's called *"Women Who Wear Antlers on their Brows"*. We, too, had stories of deer-women who grew antlers on their foreheads, and sometimes some of us could see them; they were the wise-women of our village, working with the spirit of place of our local area.

Like in all the Celtic lands, the old tales and songs tell us that long, long ago, in the Highlands our ancestors lived in a world where Sovereignty, the deer goddess, was supreme. The goddess and her priestesses were the guardians of the deer and men were, in their turn, guardians of the goddess and her herds; the hunters brought home from the fairy herd the kill designated by the goddess.

5

2012 Scotland

Figure 9: Kite Wagon, Fiona, sunrise in Glencoe

In the spring of 2012 I was able to visit the Highlands and Orkney and so remake my friendship with Elen of the Boreal Lands in those lands. I went with Fiona Dove, author and Celtic teacher, and a dear friend in the newly acquired Kite Wagon, Fiona's home-on-wheels.

Curlews & Light

Curlews! Everywhere we go we have curlews serenading us with that incredible liquid trill as they zip through the air. One did it only a couple of feet above the Kite Wagon just now.

The light up here is incredible, silvery, breath-taking. The different angle, slant the sun makes with the land this far north is a whole new world. Light defines worlds; the curve of the Earth defines worlds; the tilt of the Earth defines worlds; the distance from the sun defines worlds. To travel through the land *noticing the changes* is a part of what this road-trip is about; noticing changes is how we learn and grow. Being in the wilds makes a huge difference; it's very much harder to notice differences for light in cities, towns, villages even. In civilisation we are surrounded by human things, human noise, human lights. Out here I can write or read or see only as long as the sun gives me light. The sun is sinking fast now and will be gone soon so my writing will be ended until tomorrow. But it's later tonight than last night because we are further north. As we return south in a few days' time I shall no doubt remark that it gets darker earlier.

I love this difference. I don't want everything always to be the same. I can feel my body seething into new rhythms. My eyelids droop now and the sleepiness creeps through my body, my spirit wants me to cross over now and walk the night in dreamland.

Assynt – Meadow of Stags

In Sutherland, in the far north of Scotland, is a hamlet called Inchnadamph. The name is an anglicisation of the Gaelic name *Innis nan Damh* meaning 'meadow of the stags'. Above the meadow are the Bone Caves which contained relics of Eurasian Lynx, Brown Bear, Arctic Lemming, Arctic Fox, Brown Bear, Wolf, and, of course, Reindeer (dated to as long ago as 47,000 ago), as well as the only evidence of Polar Bears so far found in Scotland and human skeletons dated over 4,000 years ago. The caves are a designated Ancient Monument and a Site of Special Scientific Interest preserved from exploitation.

Rain. Sun. Rain
Tall mountains, deep lochs, dark moors, bright skies.
And ... deer.

Each day we go out there are deer. There in the field that leads down to the loch stands a young stag, a four-pointer, with his younger brother. They watch us walk past to go to the loch then put their heads down again to graze on the short springy turf. We are greeted.

Drizzle, but not too much, just a bit of damping as my mother used to say. I asked Elen for not too much rain, just right for the walk, and she gave it to us ... as she always does.

We went up to the glen of Allt nan Uamh. The way passes lovely waterfalls to rise steadily up into the glen. We walked silently up through heather. The place is awsome. Buzzards and a peregrine falcon overflew us; three hinds stood watching us from the other side of the glen. It felt like walking backwards in time.

We stepped back in time, some 8,000 years, as we stepped along the path. Life was so different then. As I walked I learned that I had lived in that land, in that time, walked there, worked there; I was one who led the journeymen up to the caves.

There are four caves – Badger Cave, Bone Cave, Reindeer Cave and Fox's Den. Badger Cave is the first one, we stopped to rest and feel into the place. Looking out from there the Beinn nan Cnaimhsaig looms up at you.

The Bone Cave has a small narrow passage connecting it to the Reindeer Cave. It's like a birth-passage from one world to another. I felt I would be committing myself to the Earth if I went through with no certainty of either getting through or getting back. To do this without being certain of return, to risk, to offer oneself so, would be a very worthwhile initiation. The destination is the cave of the reindeer, the all-mother deer. It would be a terrifying ordeal, scaring the shit out of me – which I think is precisely the deer lady's intention! After all, we are all mostly full of shit; to scare it out of yourself with this kind of commitment ritual once a year would be very beneficial.

The path up to the Bone Caves I walked was marked with cloven hoof-prints, I walked the deer trods.

Walking in the deer trods, walking in the footsteps of deer whose home it is fills me with a feeling I'm not sure I have easy words for. Joy comes immediately to mind but it's not enough, the feeling is more than that. There's a feeling of *life*; when my foot treads where a deer has trod some of the beast's life enters through the soul of my foot. Some of my life-energy goes out through my foot in exchange: life for life: energy for energy. The next deer who treads after me will take it in in her turn as she (or he) gives out her own life energy with each step.

It's like Olwen of the White Track – the moon lady for me. Wherever Olwen treads white petals remain in her footsteps, symbolising the energy exchange. The petals are often said to be of the thorn tree – either white or black – which she shares with Ceridwen (blackthorn) and Blodeuwedd (whitethorn).

When any of us step, walk, run, touch the Earth with our feet, we give out energy. And ... we pick up energy too, at the same time, with each step. The energy we give out is that which has passed through us and so is coloured by how we are. If we are mean and selfish, fearful for ourselves, self-centred and full of ego-stuff then the energy we give out will be small and mean with little, if any, goodness in it. If we are generous and full of joy, content with ourselves, with no personal ego problems, if we can laugh at ourselves, if we care for all life whether it's human or not, then the energy will be warm and bubbling, full of life and nourishment.

Think how it feels to you to draw in bad energy. Now think how the deer must feel. Think of drawing in lively energy ... now think of the deer again. Which would you prefer to receive? Which do you think the deer likes best?

The stags in the meadow by Loch Assynt reminded me of this. Yes, I already knew but the reminder was good ... re-mind-ers are always good, they bring things back into consciousness for us that might have got lost. They make new too, refresh; the reminder was made new for me in that moment by the deer, and their feet that trod the path before me. Thank you, Deer, Stags.

This isn't the only thing that happens as we walk the deer trods. The energy we give and receive is not only to each other. We each give and receive energy from/to the Earth herself. The energy from our footsteps goes into the Earth as we step and, as we step, we pick up Earth energy too.

The feeling I was talking about earlier is about these connections, threads of energy. Just to feel the threads is, for me, rather like walking on harp-strings, or on organ pipes as they are being played; like walking on a musical instrument, a big one with many different notes. My walking plays this great instrument. It's always been so for me; it was so for my dad too. He used to take me out walking from as soon as I could walk. We used to walk in the park and in the grounds of the ruined castle in the town where we lived. From as far back as I can remember dad would ask me who I felt had walked there before us. He meant non-human people like birds or animals that used the woodland paths, and sometimes humans too. Often we would find evidence like prints and tracks or scat, or fur, or feathers – always after I'd *felt* the path and made my pronouncement. Dad would do it too. At the time it was a game to me but I know now it was training as well, fun training, fun lessons, ones I never forgot. He called it foot-dowsing, seeing with your feet; I still call it that when I work with students.

It was foot-dowsing I did today, in the deer-trods of Inchnadamph. These are Elen's Ways, the energy roads that link and bind all things to all things, invisible and visible. Walking them with this close intent, interest, consciousness, *enables* you; it brings out your own abilities. At the same time it also enables the Earth herself.

This happens through the Spirit of Place of the place where you are – a sort of step-down from Mother Earth. Everything has spirit within it, is animate – the word animate means filled with spirit, soul, for anima means *soul*. That's the case from the smallest atom to the largest star, galaxy or universe – everything has spirit. Spirit talks to spirit. The spirit in you can (if you allow it) talk with the plant-spirit of a daisy, the rock-spirit of a stone, the bird-spirit of a sparrow, the cat-spirit of your cat, the spirit of your computer, your house, phone, car. The threads, Elen's Ways, link everything.

Walking the deer trods helps you to *know* this as it helped our long-time ancestors to know it too. They were closer then than we are now: there were fewer of them and they had not despoiled the Earth as we do now. They followed the deer trods as a normal and natural part of life and living. Nowadays we hide ourselves away from nature in great hive-cities where practically nothing in our lives is natural, it's all contrived. We are often afraid of the ways of the Earth like weather, earthquakes, volcanoes, monsoons, floods, tsunamis, winds and hurricanes, all the natural and normal patterns of the Earth and her cycles. We have driven Elen and her Ways out of our lives with our desperate need-fears that make us try to control every moment of our lives.

We will die of this fear and greed for control if we continue with it. To live we must learn again to walk the deer trods. We must learn again to give out good, free, un-fearful energy that is not bound up with our ego-wants. The sort of fearful energy many of us give out is poison to the Earth and to all her creatures, if we don't stop doing this we will die.

Deer Alchemy

Deer are wonderful animals. They are part of the ruminant tribe, beasts who have four stomachs. There are about 150 species of ruminants which include cattle, goats and sheep as well as more (to us) exotic beasts like giraffes, yaks, deer, camels, llamas, antelope. The word "ruminant" comes from the Latin *ruminare*, which means "to chew over again". Not all herbivores have four stomachs and chew the cud; for instance, horses have only one stomach.

The four stomachs correspond to the four stages of alchemy – Nigredo, Albedo, Citrinato, Rubado. Digestion is the creation of energy from matter by way of a wonderful set of chemical processes. Think about it ... turning grass into the fiery energy that enables a deer to leap an eight foot high fence ... then think about transmuting lead into gold. The transmutation – and it's *not* transformation, not changing form but changing essence – of food, of matter, into energy is an amazing process. Deer and all cud-chewers are especially good at this. Their manure is particularly good at growing vegetation, be it pasture or vegetables. This takes me to biodynamics where ruminants' manure is one of the prime ingredients of this form of gardening; nowadays we use cow manure rather than deer as it's much more readily available; [See my book **Gardening with the Moon & Stars** for more].

For thousands and thousands of years people have used every part of the deer's body to help them live. Until the last couple of thousand years this was done reverentially then, with the advent of Christianity, respect for everything not human died. Elen's Ways, the threads, the connections across the worlds, were lost to the followers of the new religion that lauded humanity over everything else. Those of us who kept and still keep the old ways alive, often in secret, also still keep respect for all life in all its wonderful diversity. Awenyddion know that humans are the youngest members of creation and are very willing to learn from their Elders.

Pig Land
Orkney means Land of the Pigs

South Ronaldsay
Strange – strange – strange ... and yet so familiar.

Today we landed on South Ronaldsay and visited the Bronze Age sweat-lodge, the Tomb of the Eagles and Banks' Chambered Cairn.

The 3,000 year-old Bronze Age sweat lodge building has a stone trough, water system and hearth, adjacent to a mound of burnt stones that were heated and put into the trough. It's just like a sweat-lodge with the deep tank at the centre for hot water and steam; the water drains out into a pool, perhaps a plunge-pool. The place is small, seating around the edge and not really any room for anything else; and the orientation is right for midwinter celebrations. We certainly had sweat-lodges in Britain, right up to the end of the 19th century, and we know from the Sami traditions that such things (saunas) were and are very much part of the Boreal traditions.

The Tomb of the Eagles is a chambered tomb sat on a cliff-top at Isbister which was discovered by accident in 1958 by local farmer, Ronnie Simison. It's about 5000 years old and contains the remains of maybe 300 people who were buried over a period of 800 years. As well as the human bones the talons and bones of 14 white-tailed sea eagles were found and dated about 4450-4000 years ago. White-tailed sea eagles became extinct in Britain in 1918. They were once common on Orkney and in recent years a few of these magnificent birds have been reintroduced.

Eagles have significance to shamans the world over; for us in the west they remind of Llew Llaw Gyffes whose totem was eagle. In Scotland he's called Lug Lamfhada but some of his exploits, such as putting out Balor's eye, remind me of Culhwch putting out the eye of Ysbaddaden Pencawr. It was Llew and his father Gwydion who hovered over me in the tomb though ... another womb from which to be birthed anew.

As I was dreaming I remembered Lot of Lothian ... the Middle Cymric name *Lleuddiniawn* – it means Region of the fortress of Lleu (Llew) – was later truncated to Lothian. Lot's wife was Morgan and her first son, Mordred, was fathered by her brother Arthur. This links across for me to Llew whose mother was

Arianrhod and his father was her brother, Gwydion. I wondered what all this was about, took it into a dream and asked.

The mother/father/son expression of triplicity is fundamental to the Celtic tradition. The twisting thread of the son-is-the-father-of-the-son; the mother weds her brother who makes her son; it goes round and round, spiralling like the triskele.

Llew and birds have a long association. Llew's own story has both the wren and the eagle in it and these two birds are linked in another story too. All the birds wanted to know which of them could fly highest and, after all the others had had their turns, it was down to the wren and the eagle. Both took off and, very quickly, only the eagle could be seen. Eventually the eagle could fly no higher; then the wren took off out of the feathers on the eagle's back and flew up a little higher still and so won the prize. It's another riddling and twisting tale which is won by the Trickster. Always, always the Trickster is central to the tale.

I still don't know what all this was about; I must still follow the deer trods to find the answer and not be impatient to find it. This kind of work doesn't respond to "tick-box syndrome", you never, never say done that, got the T-shirt, licked the stamp! It grows and grows every day.

Figure 10: Antler at Banks Tomb

Banks Tomb is quite amazing and very new. We were able to go into a chambered tomb that was still being excavated – skulls and bones still sticking out of the earth where they had originally been interred. The most incredible thing for me was to be able to actually touch a deer antler that was 5000 years old. It had been dug up only the previous month so was very new to our modern world. As I held it, felt into it, allowed the threads from the past to connect to me all sorts of images swirled up. One image in particular was of the antler being held in the hand of a awenydd and working as a conducting-rod to draw the threads within a living person and to connect them to the bones of the ancestors laid in the tomb. I kept getting the words, "Follow! Follow me!" encouraging the person to step in the spirit-deer trods and walk between worlds.

Maeshowe

The next day we went on to **Maeshowe**, perhaps one of the best known of the Orkney sites. It's an incredible place. Built on a levelled area of ground with a surrounding bank and ditch, it dates from nearly 5000 years ago. It's a winter solstice place. The sun sets directly over the Barnhouse Stone on the shortest day and its light shines directly down the passage of Maeshowe to dramatically illuminate the back wall and the passage for a few minutes. They've found the socket for a standing stone between the mound and the ditch of Maeshowe so what we see today is only a part of what was originally there.

The skill that enables people to envisage the spectacle of the setting sun at midwinter, caught in the chamber of Maeshowe, and the technical achievement of being able to create this sacred space tells us again that our ancestors were extremely knowing and sophisticated people. The thread of light reaches from the setting sun to womb of the sacred space in Maeshowe ... Elen's pathway across space linking the Earth and the Sun.

Stones of Stenness

Figure 11: Stones of Stenness

This stone circle is amazing. We walked up to them and asked permission to enter; it was granted by the spirit of place. We went in and each walked around the circle, first widdershins and then deosil, before going to the centre. And the centre is not in the middle! This is common in the old British sacred sites; if you look at the Troy Town you'll see that, in this very ancient labyrinth, its centre is not in the middle.

Nowadays we are encouraged to have quite a simplistic idea of "centre" and of "balance". Just look at these two pictures. You probably find this picture quite obviously balanced ...

Figure 12: Obvious Balance

But how about this one?

Figure 13: Balance?

Each end of the scale is very different from the other, but it is balanced.

Our ancestors had this much wider view of balance than many of us do now and incorporated it into the sacred sites they built.

Maeshowe is framed beautifully through the gap between the two "dolmen" stones at the centre of the Stenness Stones. They feel like a threshold, porch, gateway between worlds. Standing there, we both felt we were being asked to plait (braid) the stones; the stones asked us to dance them, going in and out between the stones, in both directions, like the country dance step called "the hay". We did this, to the minor consternation of a couple who had also come to see the stones, they didn't really mind and once they realised what we were doing they actually began to smile. The stones are so ancient and have been working with people for all of their lives, they reach out their threads to all of us whether we are properly conscious of it or not; they touched that couple.

Barnhouse Village

This is the next stunning place along the way … and it is a way, an energy thread marked by these sites which require something different from you before they let you pass on to the next.

Barnhouse village was discovered in 1984 by archaeologist, Dr Colin Richards. Centuries of agriculture meant little remained of the site but the excavations uncovered 15 round dwellings, probably with timber and turf roofs and turf cladding on the outer walls. It was free standing rather than encased in its own midden as Skara Brae is. Intriguingly, each building seems to have been deliberately demolished at the end of its life.

Figure 14: Barnhouse Structure Eight

The central feature of Barnhouse, Structure Eight, is surrounded by a wall with two entrances, one of which faces Maeshowe. Until the Ness of Brodgar it was the remains of the largest, covered structure from Neolithic Orkney so far discovered and is about 4,600 years old; it was built *after* all the other buildings had been abandoned. A massive hall-like structure, seven metres square with incredibly thick outer walls, it was built on a platform of yellow clay in a similar manner to Maeshowe. It has an internal courtyard of over 20 metres across. There's a large central hearth and stone dresser such as has been found in most late Neolithic houses. They also found a complete Grooved Ware pot set into the clay floor by the eastern wall which contained a treasure hoard of 14 flint nodules – flint was very scarce in Orkney.

Walking the structure, connected to the spirit of place, we felt you should go round the outer corridor in both directions, first deosil and then widdershins, making the sacred labyrinth. It felt there was water at one place where you would do the sacred purification.

Continuing on around the circle widdershins you come to the entrance to the central chamber. Here you have to cross an entrance hearth. The gate seemed likely to have been very low, meaning you would crawl in, turn right and then left – a similar reverence to going deosil and widdershins as well, possibly, as a disorienting feature so that you come to the fire-crossing really feeling you are between worlds. You cross the hearth into the huge central chamber where another firepit awaits you. This fire felt like a dancing fire, one to dance around, perhaps walking the coals again. All around the edge of the chamber is a seating platform; possibly the fire was stoked up to provide massive heat for an enormous group sweat-lodge.

We both felt it was another place to spend the winter solstice, the three days of the standstill, cleansing with water and fire, dancing, drumming, singing, storytelling, telling over the lore.

Ness of Brodgar

This is a huge and amazing place that is still being investigated now. Within it is Structure Ten an incredible and monumental structure. It's larger than Structure Eight at Barnhouse but bears a strong resemblance to it; it's built roughly east-west and points across the Harray loch towards Maeshowe.

This alignment of ritual structures along the line of the midwinter sunset emphasises the connections between them; it is the line of Sun-Return where the cycle of the year begins over again. Its siting, on the ness of Brodgar – a thin slip of land connecting one place to another – is about bridging the gap between worlds again. We travelled beyond Brodgar out to the western edge of Orkney Mainland and it is very different from one side of the Ness to the other. I feel this sacred site is about that linking and difference, bringing worlds together as well as showing how they are different – and/and again.

Ring of Brodgar

We went on to the Ring of Brodgar. It's huge, really huge, and so different again in feel. Still we were surrounded by bubbling curlews as well as larks and plovers with bunting and dippers in the lochs.

The Ring o' Brodgar is probably about 4-5000 years old but has never been properly excavated. It was built on a true circle and is thought to have originally contained 60 megaliths; only 27 remain standing now.

A *Neolithic low road* connects Skara Brae with the chambered tomb of Maeshowe, passing Stenness and Brodgar; *low roads* connect Neolithic ceremonial sites throughout Britain. Although this is a modern concept it seems to have grasped the point of "roads" connecting sites in a similar manner to the way Watkins saw them, energy threads, Elen's ways.

For years the name Brodgar has been said to be from the Old Norse brúar-garðr meaning bridge farm but Orkneyjar (the website for heritage of the Orkney islands) suggests there is another intriguing possibility. Local pronunciation is *broa(d)yeur* so could the name actually stem from *brúar-jorð* meaning *earth bridge* which would include the entire Ness o' Brodgar? My own view, from being there, is that this interpretation feels appropriate. It connects with the energy threads of Elen's ways and the concept of bridge is very strong when you actually go there, see it, cross it. How our ancestors used this bridge and the road that connects the sacred places requires much more work and lots of it won't be what is currently seen as scientific in that it won't necessarily be backed up by either previous written "facts" or material object finds. It will however be done through observation and observation was (and hopefully still is) the basis of all science ... you watch something and work it out from there, not relying on what somebody else has already written.

Journeying (done properly) is just this. You go out across worlds and/or times and observe; sometimes you also interact. You come back and collate your observations, sit with them, cogitate, ask otherworld for more to help you understand what you've done and seen. You may also be able to compare notes with friends and colleagues who have done similar journeys. *Good* science does all of these things too and is always ready for a new discovery that knocks all previous theories into a cocked hat and requires everyone to reassess their observations and ideas ... this is how we grow! This is how wisdom grows.

Nothing is static, everything is always changing. The word theory does *not* mean fact! It means our best guess with the information we currently have and as far as our minds have taken that information to date.

So we crossed the earth-bridge and followed on down the Neolithic road to Skara Brae.

Skara Brae

Skara Brae is some 4,000 years old. The buildings and their contents are incredibly well-preserved; the walls of the structures are still standing and the alleyways still roofed with their original stone slabs. The interior fittings of each house give an unparalleled glimpse of life as it was in Neolithic Orkney. Each house shares the same basic design – a large square room, with a central fireplace, a bed on either side and a shelved dresser on the wall opposite the doorway. Skara Brae was eventually abandoned to be gradually covered by a drifting wall of sand that hid it from sight for over 40 centuries.

This visit was less powerful for me. It is an amazing place and they've built a replica which you can go inside and walk through to really get the feel of the place. It was a living place rather than a ceremonial one and made me wonder about the archaeologists' classification of the stone dresser in other places as a piece of ritual furniture. Seeing it here, it felt much more like an ordinary piece of furniture, perhaps with some sacred objects on it as you do your altar at home which may be part of a larger dresser or shelf.

The place is beautiful, the northern light is stunning and the beach feels like a shore that will lead you to otherworld. We arrived early in the morning; standing on the beach and looking out to sea you face north-west so the sun was behind us, shining out onto and over the sea. We walked the beach and found someone had been there before us ... a sea otter and her cubs, the tracks were clear and new, we had missed her only by an hour or so at most!

The connection was still there though. We didn't walk in her prints but walked beside them, following where they had come up from the sea, played with a fish and eaten it, where the two cubs and rolled and play-fought in the sand. The thread was there; twining with it we could sense her telling us her story, where she'd come from, about catching the fish, what the cubs were up to, how they weren't good fishers yet themselves but getting better, even a sense of what the fish had tasted like.

Thread-twining like this is wonderful, you get so much information and, even more, you are with the beast, getting her sense of humour, how she feels about life, how it is for her right now. It's harder to twine with the cubs, they are young and deeply into getting to know thisworld rather than going across worlds as are most young ones of every species. It's one of the most beautiful gifts of Elen's ways, being able to speak with others who are not physically present at the same space-time where you are. Many folk are very interested in working with "spirit" but don't properly appreciate that spirit is in everything and not confined to Arthur Rackham's fairies, however beautiful they are. Mother Earth *wants* us to connect ... connect here in thisworld as well as across the worlds and walking the deer trods is an excellent way of doing this.

As we connect with others who are not of the human species we learn so much more, not only about them but about ourselves; we change our attitude from one of superiority (the way most of us are encouraged to see ourselves in the modern world) to realising we are younger brethren of everything else in creation. We learn to be friends with everything and this helps us learn to be friends with each other.

Sea & Sky

We went on from Skara Brae to Yesnaby Bay, a place of high, great cliffs towering over the Atlantic which reminded me of

Alma Tadema's wonderful paintings. Soft wind, bright sun, masses of seabirds – fulmars, black-backs, oyster-catchers, great skuas, gannets and, again, there were curlews galore as well as larks, bunting, swifts and swallows as well as lots of LBJs (*little brown jobs* as bird-watchers call them). We walked right round to the second bay, where two seals were basking, taking in the rays down on the rocks, it was only when they moved that we saw them they are so well camouflaged. Past the broch, we climbed up to the top of the cliffs and curled into hollows right on the edge to listen to the fantastic booming wave-caves and watch beautiful surf. Fulmars nested on those cliffs, they flew right over us, working the updrafts over our heads, screaming and diving and fishing and feeding. It was stunning.

Coming back to the Kite Wagon we saw eider ducks in the bay where the seals were, eight or nine of them, some on the sea but most on the rocks. The drakes were guarding the ducks from a hungry-looking black-back gull who eventually gave up and went off to hunt elsewhere.

Down in the first bay Fiona went to collect limpets and got a good pocket-full. We cooked them up over the fire in butter and beer, ate them with some bread and more of the Orkney Dragonhead beer. Later came the sunset … the sun sailed down the sky through all the colours of the rainbow to finally sink as a fiery crimson ball into the sea. The background-sky went through all the blues and greys and silvers, contrasting and complimenting the incredible sky-show. We sat silent, watching for a couple of hours; it was one of the most beautiful evenings of my life.

Hoy Day

Pulse Skerry beach
The next day we went to spend at a beach down by the water – from high to low – where we could sit and watch the sea and the island of Hoy across the channel.

Waves of indigo silk
Slither their way across the sands,
White lace ripples and flirts before them.

Silver-pink cloud-head
Hangs on the far side of never,
Blue beach at its edge,
Tempting.

Green lizard-head slides low
Into the indigo sea,
Drops down to stepping stones
Of rocks, calling feet ...
Will I walk there?
Yes, in the moonlight.

Waves hiss,
White lace dragon's teeth
Eating the shoreline.
Starlings fly-dance above,
Teasing.

Reindeer used to spend the winter in the soft land of Mainland back in ancient times. Grandmother deer would lead her folk down to the shore at the turn of the tide when the race is still for an hour. They swim across to Hoy for the high summer pastures. They will come back.

Hoy has high rounded hills topped with heather, good deer fodder up there. There are soft lowland meadows if needed. Even nowadays not many human folk live there. Hoy was the summer lands, Mainland was the winter lands; the alignments of the sacred places tells us this too. Working with the land and the seasons our ancestors knew how to treat her well.

Journey: The Crossing ...

I had forgotten the race.

When the tide goes out there is a terrific race between Hoy and the Mainland. When the tide is fully out the race is pretty well gone; then you can cross fairly safely. The first time I crossed I was just a few months old at the autumn return to the Mainland, for I was born on Hoy, as are we all, ready for the spring growth. That time I crossed in the middle of the herd with my mother beside me and my great aunt giving me a shove up the rear to keep going. Uncles, cousins, father too all around us young ones keeping us going, protecting us from the race. I swam and swam and swam, it felt like forever then, all of a sudden my feet touched ground and I scrambled my way up the rocks.

Winter in the lowlands was different, cold, snowy and dark at midwinter when the people celebrate the sun-return with sweat-lodges and feasting. As well as the meat from some young bucks they ferment our milk for the ecstasy drink as well as make cheese. They gift us too in return for our gifts to them. We eat the red-spotted mushroom and then the wise-women, and wise-men collect our urine to drink, to help them see the future. They are all able to walk with Great Grandmother then and see as she sees, as we see.

I grew fatter and bigger and stronger over the winter and then, in the spring, came my first return to the land of my birth. Summer is good. The bucks like me. I like the bucks. But nothing happens and Grandmother says to wait.

Comes the autumn crossing again. Now I am grown part of my job is to help those just born this spring to cross safely, as I was helped. I am given charge of two little ones; the girl is wise and strong but the boy is wild and headstrong. I try to make them obey me but the boy dashes off. He doesn't heed Grandmother shouting to him but leaps into the sea too early, the race has not yet died down enough. At first he swims strongly, proud of himself, then the race catches him and he is swept away. I hear him calling, calling, calling until he is gone under and the sea has swallowed him. After we all land safely I hear him calling in my dreams. I will not forget.

Reality, Spirit & Death

Nowadays, how many folk know that a full grown lobster is 140 years old? Can you eat history? The ear-bones of cod show growth-rings like a tree. A six foot long cod – and how many of those are there nowadays? – will be 100 years old, and cod don't breed until they're thirty years old so, when you order cod-n-chips, you're likely eating one of the few baby cod that are still around. Our ancestors knew all this ... most of us nowadays don't even know that we don't know it.

Learning Elen's ways will help you learn about all the life we share this beautiful planet with.

However Elen appears to you, learn from her. In the lands of the Boreal Forest we have all the threads to reach out and touch, hold and learn from *but* we have to reach out to her. Elen will never force us to see or to learn, not until we ask her to show us, so it's up to us to ask.

Asking is about just that, asking, but it has more to it as well ... if you ask you *will* be answered. To hear the answer you must learn to listen.

Listening means letting go of your personality-ego, your own personal needs and wants to be noticed, to be important – all the things people seem to be encouraged to push to the front nowadays. To listen we have to move out of being personality-centred.

Once you start to get into the habit of *not* being centred in the small personal-self, once you regularly move to centring in the spirit-self, you will find your ability to listen increases and you get better at it. Putting the little personal-self out of the way like this is integral to spirit-keeper practice. It's also part of growing up – you cease to be the centre of your universe. This helps you to allow more *reality* into your life. TS Eliot, in his poem Burnt Norton, rightly says, "*Humankind cannot bear very much reality*"; this is so true. This inability to listen has, in my opinion, grown exponentially since we began serious farming. For a long while we kept a reasonable hold on reality, the human population did not begin to increase to impossible levels for several thousand years. We still felt the interconnectedness of all things. We knew that stones, plants, trees, animals, birds, insects, the very Earth herself all know far more about how to live well than we do … and we still knew how to ask them to show and help us, we knew that they are our elder brethren. This all got horribly lost with Christianity which told us to believe that humanity is the pinnacle of creation rather than new-boy-on-the-block. Awenyddion, shamans, of all lands still know and remember this.

Understanding that you are actually *not* the best thing since sliced cat-food means your ego does *not* get dented by asking. It means you don't feel you have to be able to fix everything. It means you are likely to consider what most people call *inanimate objects* to be as important as yourself. Consider how this attitude changes your ideas of what you will throw away. It also means you are willing to share your food with the fox and the leopard, knowing that they too are hungry. Think about how I learned about the life of the otter on the beach at Skara Brae, I knew she was no longer hungry because she had caught a fish, I would have similarly known if she was hungry … I would have felt her sensations and feelings in my own body, known her like I know my own flesh. This is how Elen's ways work. Living this way you completely lose the "them and us" attitudes most people have.

Nature is not competitive. The old, the weak and the young are indeed often food for others; plants are food for animals, birds, fish and insects as well as humans. The wholeness of Lovelock's Gaia feeds and nourishes herself with nothing wishing to live forever.

As far as I know humans are the only species that broods on death or fears old age. All our elder brethren grow old and die with relative grace. For the past sixty-plus years cats have shared my life; come the end they have often gone off to find a peaceful place to quietly slip away and die. I have been privileged to be with three of them, able to watch with them as their spirit slips out of their Earth-shell. I have also watched while several human-friends have done the same thing. I completely disagree with Dylan Thomas who speaks of fighting the dying of the light. To me, his attitude speaks of the childish personality that has no concept of reality, let alone any connection with the divine.

Walking the deer trods across to the Isles of the Dead is the way for me. In Britain so many of our western isles are called *summer lands* and *isles of the dead*; we follow the sun down into the west to rise up again in the dawning of a new incarnation.

Journey: Death

Sitting here on the beach at Pulse Skerry, the western shores of Orkney Mainland, looking across to the shores of Hoy I am following the Grandmother deer as she leads the herd down to the water's edge at the slack of the tide. It's barely a mile to swim and the currents are at their softest.

'Now!' she says as into the water she walks. We follow.

The cold takes the breath away at first but my legs are soon moving, swimming me over. The huge herd is all around me, the strongest at the edges and the men who live with us in the long coracles alongside them. They catch the straying ones and push them back into the herd.

An old one lags behind. I hear his laboured breathing, slow, slow, and sense his spirit fly up as his body sinks below the waves. Crabs and lobsters and fish will eat well of his body for a few days. He is glad to be of service to his fishy brethren. I will not see him again until I, too, pass into the Summerland.

Now my swimming feet touch sand and gravel. I scrabble hooves and push, jump, leap out of the water onto the new land. I stand a moment, shake myself, a mist of water flies out from my coat and mane. I jump for the new grass of the low meadow.

Grandmother walks on into the pasture, stands a moment, counting threads as she counts us all. Most of us have made it but three are now fish-food and one body has been dragged ashore for the men to eat. All is well. All is very well. Tomorrow we will lead the human people up into the high pastures.

Up in the high pastures the sun never sets at midsummer. At midday the sun is bright and hot, burnishing the sky and our backs. At midnight the light is soft, crepuscular, creeping into shadows but never gone. The food is good and plentiful. Up here, this high, there is always a breeze keeping the summer midges away. If we were lower down now we would be plagued with flies but here the air is good.

I feel a spring in my step, my antlers grow, I cavort on the hilltops. Grandmother chuckles, she has seen it all before. The young bucks watch me, sometimes give me a nip; I kick back but I'm noticing several ... we'll see, we'll see, will Grandmother approve my mating this year? Do I wish to mate? The freedom to run still flows in my blood, is the mating ecstasy better than that? I do not know. I will wait, listen to Grandmother. Many generations of us has she watched over, she knows, I will listen.

I am here again, on the seashore in my own human form. The oyster catchers come down as the tide goes out exposing the rock pools where they hunt and fish. Fluttering wings, delicate flight, landing softly on the seaweed-covered rocks, piping to each other ... evensong.

The curlew bubbles and trills, disturbed for a moment from

her hunting by the black-and-white evening-comers. Soon she is quiet again, walking, hunting her own food.

The rocks are exposed now. The reef at the end catches the waves, making them boom and thunder, then they hiss away, slithering back into the ocean to come again, a moment later. The dance of waves and rocks; a place of meetings and partings, every moment made anew, then gone only to come again, but differently. *Plus ca change, plus c'est la meme chose* – everything changes, and only so does everything remain.

Elen's ways lead us back to knowing this and to living this. Only so will humankind survive. The art of letting go, of not knowing best, of being full of expectancy but without expectations ... this is walking the deer trods.

6

Following the Deer Trods

Following the deer trods is to open yourself to Elen's complex, multiple and beautiful ways.

The path of the awenydd follows the numinous threads that form and hold the body of the Earth. We know them as threads, energy lines, ley lines, song lines, dragon lines. Sometimes they are straight, sometimes sinuous. They can appear in all colours but many humans often see them as silvery. They underlie footpaths, roads and tracks; follow rivers and streams, and are the currents in the ocean.

The universe we live in, like all universes, *is* spirit. Elen's Ways happen within our own bodies and within the bodies of all creation including rocks and mountains, planets and galaxies; in fact they are everywhere throughout the whole universe. In our own bodies they link the major and minor energy centres that we may know better as the chakras. In the Earth they link the sacred places. Scientists currently call them *string-theory* and *dark matter* too.

Growing up with Elen

I grew up with Elen and have been working with her all my life as a practising awenydd, learning my craft from my father and uncles, and from the wise women of the village.

The next-door neighbour was a healer and the village midwife; she also did the laying out of the dead so she was a transition lady, a doorkeeper and holder of the thresholds of birth and death. We youngsters would be detailed to help her with both births and deaths so I grew up knowing that birth and death are two sides of one coin, that coming into thisworld is leaving otherworld and vice versa. As far as birthing goes I suspect most people have some idea of it and many of you will have children of your own. Hot water, towels, care, comfort and help are the main things. I'm talking back in the 1950s now, you only went into hospital if it looked dangerous; the doctor would come round to help if necessary but the work was all down to the midwife ... and her assistants, the village children including me.

In those days, in my village, it was normal that when a person died the doctor would come and pronounce death, sign a certificate and then the midwife would take over with preparing the body before the undertakers were called. Funeral parlours were expensive, you only used them for the things that you couldn't do yourself and, besides, it was much nicer for a friend to look after your body when you had passed over, someone who knew you and knew what rituals needed to be done.

After death, the first thing we did was the washing. The midwife or one of the older girls prepared the water; it was something I did later after I passed puberty. We used Elder-water. First the leaves were steeped overnight in the water from the village sacred well then, next morning, we would boil up elderberries in the water. If fresh berries weren't available (as was often the case) we used Elder vinegar made over the autumn. Either way the washing water came up a beautiful wine-colour. We all got to know what old and dead bodies looked like and not to be afraid of them nor of the process of death.

In those days the sacred well that gave us the water was owned by my aunt. She and my gardening uncle lived in the well-cottage with the well itself set in the wall between our garden and theirs. In those days there was a pump on the well so you could draw the water but that's all gone now.

While we youngsters did the water-wash for the corpse the midwife prepared the smoke. The smoke-wash was an incense bath for which the midwife would choose which herbs to use depending on the person and the season. We children would get sent out the day before to find them, many of our parents grew them in the garden but some came from the hedges.

There would be other offerings from family and friends, and other rituals that we children didn't go to until we were older, after puberty. These rituals often involved singing (we called it "Enchanting") and sitting with the body. Sometimes people would do a form of drumming, using stones or woodblocks, and hawk bells, I've seen folk knocking horse brasses together too. It was all about conversing with the spirit that had recently inhabited the body, making sure all was as it should be before giving the body back to the Earth. Relatives would come to do this, chatting with the spirit until it had moved on.

The burial or cremation would happen after the spirit had fully left the body, usually after three days. Back in the 1950s the bodies were kept at home for the 3 days, often on the dining room table if there was a dining room, in the coffin. Village folk and relations would come to pay their respects during that time.

Sometimes there would be problems. In one ritual we were helping this man who had been killed in a fight. It was quite an effort because it was actually he who had started the fight and he needed to make his peace with the other man who was badly injured and unconscious in hospital. It was very hard work and took some organising. We did it by somebody (me) being volunteered to do a hospital visit to sit with the other man while I was also connected to the group by the corpse and transmit between them. This sort of thing just doesn't allow one to have the usual misconceptions about death.

I dropped out of the circle when I left home to go to university in 1966/7. The next time I was involved in one of those rituals was at the death of my father in 1991 and then the death of my stepmother in 1993. Both their rituals were much shorter and the body washing was all gone by then, taken over by the local undertakers which I found strange and disconnected. I was able to do the sitting-with rituals with them both though which was very good.

This is just one part of how I grew up, the sort of rituals that were natural and normal for me. I've followed these and other paths learned in childhood all my life.

Walking Between Worlds

It's fascinating to walk between worlds, between times, I've done it all my life; so did my father and mother, aunts and uncles, so it's a natural part of life and living. From a lifetime of talking to people I think many of us do this but, because of things like "being normal", conforming, fitting in with other people's views, political correctness not seeming odd, etc, etc, they are afraid to say that they do. I've experienced this need to "stuff" my reality in order to gain acceptance and approval – it's a frightful thing. It is however very much part of the way we live nowadays. Think about it for yourself; how often do you say something you don't believe, which isn't true for you, in order not to give offence? It's something to grow out of, stop doing. Stuffing yourself means you lose the connection with Elen's Ways.

Elen's Ways are multifunctional, like our modern fibre-optic cables that can carry phone, TV, radio, all that stuff, all at the same time. The threads, Elen's Ways, run throughout the Earth. Alfred Watkins saw them as straight, a silver web of pathways criss-crossing the land linking places together. From my own experience I'd say this is *part* of the picture: there are straight lines and there are curving, twisting and spiralling lines – *both*, not either/or but *and/and*, different styles of thread carry things differently. I learned in childhood from the wise folk of the village that the threads are complex and multiple and, as I grow older, I come to differentiate them more and more.

Perhaps a good way to describe this learning is that it's similar to learning to hear an orchestra. At first it's a noise, a pleasant noise probably with a strong tune in places that stands out but you're not able to hear details. As you go to more concerts, listen more, you find yourself knowing strings from wind; more practice and you find you can tell woodwind from brass; still more practice and you can do violins from cellos and basses. Eventually you can hear, differentiate, the 1st violin from the other violin players and even recognise who the conductor is. Getting to Elen's Ways is like that. You can sense them, maybe see them, in a general way at first. As you walk them more and more so you learn to know between the different things the carry ... and do, and are. It takes lots of practice, in fact you never stop learning, but it's great fun.

When people don't allow you your own way of seeing, when they tell you the threads are one particular way while you can see that they're also another, it can be very off-putting and confusing. The modern trend, even among some pagans, for the old "country ways" to be taken over by academics and shoved into an academic box, pigeonhole, category, is not good for real practice or for those wanting to learn the old ways. It's worth remembering that even Mircea Eliade was a philosopher – not a shaman himself – and that he was *watching*, not participating and certainly not a celebrant; and he was one of the best of the academics to look at shamanic ways. He wrote books *about* what he observed, which is good scientific practice. They tell of what he saw, thought, what he pieced together from watching from the outside *not* about what he knew in his bones from actually living it because he didn't do that.

We are so conditioned to believe whatever is said by someone with alphabet soup after their name that we forget, and lose all confidence in, our own minds and intuition; we have no practice in using either. We are conditioned out of questioning. One who wishes to follow Elen's Ways must learn to question ... only by questions and by finding your own answers to these questions will you find your way along the deer trods.

Following the multifunction threads leads you deeper than you may even dream of at the beginning of your journey; and that journey won't stop even after you die.

Elen's threads cross time and space. This is how I journey back in the lands to find out about places and peoples and the spirits of place. I've been fortunate in that, many times, I've been able to find other evidence to corroborate my journeys. A journey in 2011 on Exmoor took me through a very ancient forest of huge pine trees which does not exist in the everyday world. Subsequent research showed that, some 8000 years ago, there was indeed a deep pine forest on that part of Exmoor. That's the sort of thing that happens; it did for my father too.

Dad was a major influence on my early life. My birth-mother died when I was three and a half years old so we had very little time together. I still remember her though and she has been in my life as a companion all the years since puberty. Dad involved me in everything he was doing from de-coking the car, making a concrete floor for the conservatory, gardening and building projects around the house, walking the countryside, philosophy and working with spirit. All of it was normal and part of everyday life for me as a child. This is a very good way to learn. Some pagan parents believe the child shouldn't experience shaman life and ritual until they're "old enough" ... whenever that might be. Dad wasn't like that. I could always say I didn't want to do something but the things we did were so interesting I always wanted to do them, even as a rebellious teenager. When exploring and discovery has been the bread of life as long as you can remember you don't want to stop. It wasn't what people would call a normal childhood, I didn't enjoy the things normal kids did but those of us whose parents were awenyddion found we had little in common with those who knew nothing of the old ways. We quickly learned not to talk about it outside the village unless we knew we were with others from cunning families. And mostly we never had any urge to show off our "magic" powers ... we knew very well how that might end!

Listening to the Elders

Another awenyddion practice is that of listening to the elders. The old folk who talked to me and taught me knew what they knew.

How do you get to be an elder? Well, first off, there's no degree in it, Indeed having a degree might actually exclude being one if the degree is part of your *armour propre*, your own vision of who you are, rather than a handy add-on that has been useful to you in a practical (and preferably not a money-grubbing) way. Elders have *lived their lives*, they've seen things, made mistakes and are willing to talk about those mistakes and so help you; often they've made wonderful things too and will show you how to do so yourself. Elders come about because of the respect others feel for them and for how they live their lives. You don't call yourself an elder ... but other people do.

Elders have followed the deer trods, walked Elen's paths through their lives as well as through the land; they look for and see the wisdom in the land, in animals, birds, trees, fish, insects; they listen to their elder brethren ... the rest of creation.

Deer Stalking – Working with Elen

Currently stalking has a lot of bad press as it is connected with people stalking each other for emotional reasons and often ending up in very nasty situations. Over history though it has had a different interpretation, to stalk is to follow, trail, track and hunt something, usually an animal or bird for food or, nowadays, with a camera for photography. To do this means you must learn all you can about the creature you want to follow.

Stalking Elen is about following, trailing and tracking her to ask for nourishment, spirit-food rather than physical food. Some people have been known to stalk her in the hopes of getting power for themselves; they invariably come to a bad end. It's one of the laws of spirit that you get back what you give out, if your motives are selfish then you will get selfishness returned to you.

When you stalk Elen you follow her deer-trods and you need to use all the subtle skills of stalking a real, physical deer in order to do so. She will test you day in, day out, to see how you are doing, if you have the stamina to run the course, if you have the nous and gumption to learn from your mistakes … if you can keep up with her.

Spirit Keeper …
My uncle was a woodsman. He used to take me out into the woods or up onto the moor as part of the spirit-keeper ways he taught me as a little child. We would often go out at dusk and not come back until maybe gone midnight. There were special places we frequented, under trees, beside brooks, hunched up in the heather, under rocks and in caves. We would go, with a thermos and maybe a sandwich, to sit and watch. Dormice would come right down to us, bats, owls, stoats and weasels, badgers and

foxes, rats and moles and mice.

Uncle Jack would whisper to me about them and, because he was a real *wild man*, they would come right up to his hand; they knew he knew them and they trusted him. I've seen him with an adder coiled round his wrist of an afternoon in summer, the pair of them, man and snake, dozing in the sun, doing each other no harm. Other times I've seen him call down a wild falcon or hawk to his wrist; he would talk to the bird and sometimes, on occasion, the bird would allow me to stroke her before she flew off. I've called owls down to me, myself.

I know other people who can do this. And I know too that we, every one of us, could learn to do this if we wished but it's hard work to learn if you weren't brought up to it as I was from babyhood. But it's still by no means impossible to learn.

Many wild habitats are unique and occur only in that place so those who live there need specialised local knowledge to know them and how to live and work in them. Uncle was one of those sorts of people.

Hunter-gatherers live where they do at least partly because they know their land and know how to live in it; they are intimately linked to their land. Citification and easy transport have taken these abilities away from most people in the world today so when they go out into the countryside they rely on what other people tell them rather than knowing the natural world in their own bones. Those of us who still live the old ways are not so dependent on other people, we learned in our childhoods how the non-human world works and how it can help us, and we teach it on to our own children.

Even in such places as the boreal forest, there is a lot of variation in the plants, animals and in the local landscape. Knowing your way around means you need to build a 3D map in your mind and this takes time, it means actually going out in the land on your own feet rather than driving round it in a car; not sitting indoors looking at pictures nor yet relying on your GPS system or your mobile phone. Even a map – although it's a wonderfully useful bit of kit – will not give you the *feel* of actually walking the land herself; walking the land and sleeping out, if you can, will get that knowing of her into your bones.

It's a part of following the deer trods. In their physical form these are the animal trails, pathways, ancient roads and migration routes that are thousands and thousands of years old. They are ways our ancestors followed when they too were hunter-gatherers. Following the trails, the paths, the deer trods, will gradually show you about the spirit of place where you live, and the spirits of place that you visit.

Bushcraft

Bushcraft is about being confident and comfortable in the natural environment. *(Tony Bristow of BCUK)*

I'm a Bushcraft person and one of the things it can teach you is *"Carry less by knowing more"* *(quote from Wayland at Ravenlore)*. This is one of the things I was taught by the awenyddion who brought me up, it works just as well for shamans as it does for bushcrafters.

Unlike Harry Potter you do not need a load of kit in order to follow the old ways but you do need a load of *nous*, knowing. This is about *knowing* the land where you live *and* knowing how to ask the land for help. Asking – the ability and skill so to do – is fundamental to the old ways. The Land herself, the rocks and stones and soil, the ancestors, the trees, plants, insects, bugs, creatures and beasts will all help you … if you ask. If you don't ask, they won't; likely then you'll end up in a right old mess!

When you do ask you have to be prepared to listen … as this story from Wayland illustrates very well …

Finding Your Way

by Wayland at Ravenlore

I was once on a hillside in the early evening, preparing some food, when a party of walkers approached me, led by a flustered looking gentleman with a map and compass in his hand.

They looked well equipped for the hill, expensive goretex jackets, trekking poles, the lot. The only problem was that they were on the wrong hill.

It would seem that they had parked in the wrong car park. Following their leader's compass they had then taken the wrong path.

Following this wrong path they had walked all the way to the wrong peak and then got lost when the wrong path down, took them in the wrong direction and then suddenly disappeared in the wrong place.

They had been walking all day without a clue as to where they actually were.

When I pointed out their actual position on their map, at first they refused to believe me. I eventually had to dig out a handheld GPS that was in the bottom of my bergen and then the "leader" said the GPS must be wrong.

I asked them where they thought their cars were and they pointed to the map. I asked them again, more carefully, where in this landscape they had parked the cars. They looked at me blankly. I asked where they had walked down from. They pointed at three different peaks.

At this point I decided to walk them down from the hill myself.

The point to this story is that the map is not the land. The compass bearing is not the way and the GPS co-ordinate is not your location. They are all useful representations of these things but they are not actually these things.

I'm certainly not saying you should not use these things when outdoors, but I am saying you should learn to navigate without them at times.

Batteries and electronics fail, even compasses are thrown off by objects in your kit or even in the landscape, and maps get blown away in the wind.

I've seen all these things happen and, if you do not know how to read the landscape and the signs around you, then you can quickly become very lost.

The most reliable guide you have is the land itself. Unlike some other signs it will not quickly change.

Look at the landscape as you walk through it. Work out where on the horizon you are heading and look back to see where you have come from. As you look around, remember objects or features that you will be able to see if you have to retrace your steps. Look at the relationship between your route and these features and make notes if you need them.

Being in the habit of doing these things will mean that if you lose your navigation equipment or the mist closes in, you will have a good mental picture of the landscape that will be an enormous help in getting you home in one piece.

These are things you should do even if you are using navigational aids, as you should be able to fit this information to what you can see on your map and compass. If you can't make it fit, stop, take a break and consider if you are actually where you think you are.

If you are navigating with just a GPS then retrace your steps to a city and do not enter the wilderness again until you have bought a good map and compass. Mountain rescue teams have enough to do without having to recover corpses with failed GPS units.

Wayland is so right. And not only about hiking. These self-same things happen to you in your work with spirit. You read a book, take a course, learn a load of spells and set off on your spirit-journey believing you are following the deer trods. You have all the right spirit-clobber and kit plus a head-full of knowledge and absolutely no idea how to use it ... all the gear but no idea as we say in bushcraft.

To work in spirit you must go slowly, learn the lie of the land in which you work, meet the otherworldly beings, learn to ask them for help and learn to listen properly to what they show and tell you. You really will find yourself up shit creek without a paddle if you start telling an otherworldly being that their spirit GPS is wrong!

To stalk Elen – and she loves to be stalked – you need to learn to be canny, how to ask and how to listen. And you must go slowly and learn her land … the Earth.

Tracking

Tracking Elen through spirit and across the worlds is like tracking an animal in the woods, moors, riverside and desert. You need the same skills, the same nous and the same ability for patience, observation, silence and being quiet and invisible that you need to find a deer or a pine marten or a dormouse.

I'm fortunate to know some superb trackers. One of them, Paul Kirtley of Frontier Bushcraft, is a passionate tracker. Even when he's just out for a leisurely walk in the woods he's looking for tracks and sign left by animals. Paul says, *"Once you start looking, there are signs of animal activity everywhere… In fact, after you tune in to the evidence of wildlife activity in your local woods and fields, you'll certainly see tracks and sign of animals a lot more frequently than [you see] many of the animals themselves."*

Paul says *after you tune in* – there's the thing. Tuning in, getting on the thread, being aware of all the Life around you, this is the way of the tracker and stalker. Life has so much to show and tell you if you are willing to listen and learn. Even when you don't actually see the animal, looking at the sign they have left behind gives fascinating insights into their lives.

To the awenydd tracking is a sacred responsibility. I am very aware that I am a visitor into the lives and homes of the creatures whose land I pass through. I treasure the gift they give me in allowing me to be with them, to watch them; I respect them and do my best not to intrude. If I intrude I can cause serious damage and disturbance to them, like making them abandon their young. I could disturb their nesting grounds, damage feeding places and might even cause an animal's death. In winter, for instance, many animals find it very hard to gather enough energy to stay alive each day; wasting energy to escape from me could rob them of so much energy so that they die of exhaustion and starvation. I will not do that.

Animal Tracks and Sign

by Paul Kirtley ...

I've seen roe deer in these woods before. A few years back, while I was sitting quietly, a doe and her two almost full-grown youngsters almost walked into me. It was a wonderful experience. Today I wasn't so lucky to have even a glimpse of deer but there were signs of their presence. There was a faint deer trail through the leaves and I found some droppings on it but they weren't so fresh. Roe deer droppings are quite small, cylindrical, often with one end pointed and one end indented. When they are fresh they are black and shiny, later becoming brown and matt.

Further along I found a laying-up area where an animal had rested. Roe are a little unusual amongst deer as they tend to scrape away leaves and vegetation, preferring to lay on bare earth. The resting places of other species such as fallow are often observed as just a deer-shaped flattening of leaves or vegetation. There is a disturbance to the leaves under the bush. You can spot this from a distance as a dark patch compared to the overall shade of the ground cover in the area.

Further on still I found fresh disturbance on some steep ground which an animal had traversed and here there were also some droppings that were quite fresh. Shortly after this point, the trail disappeared into a dense thicket of rhododendron.

Several species of animal will take bark off trees for food, particularly in winter. When trying to work out which species of animal has removed the bark, think about what the height of the damage suggests about the size of the animal. For example a deer can reach higher than a rabbit. As well as an animal's stature, also consider abilities of various animals – for example squirrels will climb up and bark trees high up. Look for other sign of animals nearby – for example rabbit runs, deer racks, droppings, fur or hair, other feeding sign or anything else that corroborates your suspicions.

There were rabbit runs under a nearby fence and evidence of their digging in the immediate area.

As you learn more about animal behaviour this knowledge will also help differentiate between similar damage made by different species. For example, deer and sheep are both ruminants and both have two incisor teeth at the front of their lower jaw and a hard palate replacing their upper incisors; when deer bark trees they tend to insert their (lower) incisors and then strip the bark by running their teeth vertically up the trunk of the tree, whereas sheep tend to work more across the axis of the trunk, giving the appearance of nibbling rather than stripping. Also note wool caught on nearby low branches.

Badgers

The other day we came across a badger sett under a hawthorn hedge halfway up a hillside of moderate slope – classic positioning for a badger's home. Later on in the woods, down near a stream, we found fresh evidence of badgers feeding from a rotten tree stump. The mossy turf had been pulled back, the earth dug and the stump raided for grubs.

Owl Pellets

Not long before dusk we were walking through a mature conifer plantation. We came into an area populated by mature larches, lofty and well-spaced with a mossy under-storey. We stopped for a brew and nearby there were a couple of owl pellets. Owl pellets are a mass of regurgitated indigestible material that does not pass through the owl's gut. The contents of the pellet give you a very good idea of what the owl has been feeding on. You can clearly see bones amongst their contents.

The size, shape and contents of the pellet also gives a good indication of which species of owl might have produced it. This is something I'm by no means an expert in but my deduction, based on the uneven nature of the surface of the pellet and the number of bones showing and protruding, is that these pellets were produced by a tawny owl. They were quite long though so I also considered whether they might have been produced by a long-eared owl based on descriptions in my field guide.

Tracking and being Awenydd

What you see depends on what you're looking at and where you're looking from.

At first glance, Paul's descriptions of things to take note of in tracking might not seem to have any relevance to spirit keeping … but they do. Paul is not only a very observant person he is also experienced in understanding what he's looking at and used to asking himself auxiliary questions which will expand his understanding.

The most important thing he looks for is differences, changes. He takes his time and observes where he is, notices its overall colour and shape, then he spends time observing where there are patches of difference.

As you work as awenydd you will learn to do this with all of your life – your home, your job, your journey to work, your relationships, everything. Remember, everything is spirit, some of it is very solid and what we know as "everyday", this is likely the part you're most used to. You probably know that the colour spectrum in which our human eyes see; the rainbow colours, the spectrum of visible light, is just a tiny wee bit of the overall electromagnetic spectrum. The universe we live in is like that, spirit is even more huge than the electromagnetic spectrum; it includes the everyday world we're used to but this is just a tiny wee bit of the whole of spirit, like the rainbow colours our physical eyes can see.

To learn to observe life, the universe and everything is what the awenydd does. She or he learns to see differences in it as the tracker does and gradually to understand what these difference show and tell. If you begin to teach yourself something relatively easy like looking for animal signs when you go out for a walk you can then transfer these skills to your life as an awenydd, a spirit keeper, a shaman. This is how I was taught as a child by the woodwise awenyddion of my family and the village.

My practice doesn't come from "core shamanism", it hasn't been reinvented or any of the other terms that seem common in some circles. It comes from my awenydd family, the village and the land where I grew up, from the places I've lived and where I live now as well as the places I've visited; it comes from people who are rooted in the customs of land.

Journey-work

Take some time each week to go out into the natural world and walk there, go slowly, watch the path, stop and look at things as you pass, a bit of wool caught on a bramble perhaps or animal droppings – what are they? What do they tell you about the animal they come from and what s/he ate, how healthy they were? Begin to learn the tracks and footprints, of animals – there are lots of good books to help you – so you know who has passed this way. After a while you'll learn to know how old they are so you can see the last time a fox, say, passed down this track, as well as what s/he had for dinner and whether there are cubs.

Take some time to just sit for a couple of hours under a tree or bush. You have to learn to be very still to do this and nowadays children are not taught that as I was when I was a little kiddie; but you *have* to be still and quiet if you want animals to come close to you. This means learning to relax your muscles properly; to be warm which means wearing appropriate clothing, as does being as nearly invisible as you can. It means learning to take something warm to sit on, camping sleep-pads are good and very light, they stop the heat being sucked out of you by the cold ground. It means learning to move very slowly and softly; again who teaches their children to do this nowadays? More often the children are encouraged to be loud and boisterous – and so they never see any animals as the beasts are long gone before the children ever get there. If you've not been trained in being slow, careful, quiet and invisible then it will take you some time to learn ... but it's *so* worth it. Once you begin to be able to move quietly in the woods, fields, moorlands, beach, cliffs, you will see far more of your non-human neighbours. They see you all the time – and avoid you – but once you are able to be quiet and still they will venture out and you will come to know them.

Non-Human Neighbours

In human terms we are often encouraged, and want to, know our neighbours; there's lots of talk of "community" in cities and towns and villages but what about our non-human neighbours?

Do you know all the non-human beasties you share your house with? Probably not; and quite possibly your skin just crawled as you read those words. We're told by every authority figure nowadays that bugs and insects and rodents and pigeons and birds and ... and ... and ... are all dangerous, carry germs and parasites and are bad for our health or will steal our food, or will bite our children. I'm afraid I have to say poppycock! If you actually think about the people who tell you all this, and then think about what axe they may have to grind, it really helps to get a different perspective on our non-human neighbours.

For instance: bugs carry germs; said by a "health official", who has a job in health, that job is partly paid for by (say) pharmaceutical companies; so this health official's salary is partly (if not wholly) paid for by people who need you to buy their products to keep their company alive. The health official may well have a mortgage and so needs his salary to keep up payments on his home, and to pay for food for himself, his kids, partner, etc. And so on, and so on. Our modern, citified lives tend to push us away from asking too many questions in case those questions cause us to think and so, in turn, question why we do things … like kill all bugs. We don't go out and discover for ourselves what bugs are where, what those bugs do, if, when and how they might be dangerous to us and, most importantly what our own part in them becoming dangerous is. We've lost all sense of interconnection.

Getting to know our non-human neighbours helps to bring this sense of interconnection back. We become connected to the deer trods, the pathways of our elder brethren, as our ancestors were.

I'm not suggesting we give up flushing toilets, washing machines, the internet, mobile phones or computers, or anything like that. The *and/and* approach is far more beneficial than the *either/or* one; *and/and* is inclusive where *either/or* is exclusive. We can have all those things and still be connected to all the life around us our non-human neighbours … but being connected will change how with think of and use all our modern conveniences.

Ancestral Nous & Spirits of Place

We're used to seeing "native peoples" on TV, in foreign lands but we practically never realise that *we are native here*, at home in our own lands, wherever those lands may be. Until we feel native, feel that we are a part of the land where we live, we disconnect ourselves from our ancestral knowing and nous. I'm hoping this book will help you remember the old ways within you.

Always, the people who know the land best are the local people who spend time in the land, its forests and its waters. And there are still folk in Britain who do this, have this nous and are willing to help you find it in yourself.

Learning the old skills, how to live in the woods, how plants can help you, which plants you can eat, which will heal your wounds; learning to whittle a tent peg or a wooden spoon; cooking wild food; all this draws your vision back to the ancestral ways of the deer trods. Just sleeping out with your ear against the Mother's breast, watching the stars, hearing the wildlife that comes out after darkness falls, and watching the dawn come and the sun rise over the horizon with no human habitation in sight, all these give you a whole new perspective on life, the universe and everything. They bring you closer to Elen of the Ways.

Getting to Know the Ancestors

One of the best ways of bringing yourself nearer to the Old Ones is to spend some time working to their timetable and lifestyle. This way you come to see the world through *their* eyes – rather than the eyes of romantic imagination that many modern shamanic paths seem to imbue.

See if you can just go wild-camping on your own for a couple of days. Take some food and shelter, don't go too far on your first trip but stay out all night without any human company. Make sure you'll be warm enough – sleep in your clothes as well as the sleeping bag, take something to lie on so you don't lie directly on the ground as this will suck the warmth from your body; try to take an easy and safe form of fire with you for ritual and comfort as well as cooking food and making a hot brew. It is so, so different sleeping out with nature, scenting the earth and the plants, hearing the quick rustle of the night-beasts, waking to the dawn sky.

It will walk you through all your indoctrinated fears of the dark, of "wild animals", of being alone. And it will open you to sensing the Earth herself, the deer goddess, as you lie on her breast. If you are able to camp somewhere there are deer – and that's lots and lots of places throughout Britain – then you might have a wonderful experience as Paul Kirtley did with the roe deer, or as I did with the red deer hind. Being out, *alone*, in a wild place will enable you to begin to know your brethren of the animal kingdom and know them as friends and brothers rather than something to be afraid of.

Fear is so destructive. We are taught to fear almost everything and yet nothing except other human beings is likely to harm us or has harm in their heart. Learning to remember that all of creation is our brother is vital for the awenydd.

We don't get taught things like this nowadays, we miss out on so much!

You can learn masses from owl pellets or fox scat in the woods near your home, even London and city parks are full of the non-human neighbours you share the world with.

Walking the deer trods is to learn how close we are to nature and to everything in the beautiful world we share with our non-human brethren. This shows us how we are connected to everything whether or not it appears inanimate and this is what the awenydd knows.

Elen of the Ways can be your mentor, teacher and guiding spirit as she is mine. She will always be here for you to call on if you need. You will find her everywhere.

MOON

BOOKS

Moon Books invites you to begin or deepen your encounter with Paganism, in all its rich, creative, flourishing forms.